First World War
and Army of Occupation
War Diary
France, Belgium and Germany

40 DIVISION
119 Infantry Brigade
Welsh Regiment
18th Battalion.
13 June 1915 - 17 June 1918

WO95/2607/2

The Naval & Military Press Ltd
www.nmarchive.com
Published in association with The National Archives

Published by

The Naval & Military Press Ltd

Unit 10 Ridgewood Industrial Park,

Uckfield, East Sussex,

TN22 5QE England

Tel: +44 (0) 1825 749494

www.naval-military-press.com

www.nmarchive.com

This diary has been reprinted in facsimile from the original. Any imperfections are inevitably reproduced and the quality may fall short of modern type and cartographic standards.

© **Crown Copyright**
Images reproduced by permission of The National Archives, London, England, 2015.

Contents

Document type	Place/Title	Date From	Date To
Heading	WO95/2607/2		
Heading	18th Bn Welsh Regt Jun 1916-Jun 1918		
War Diary	Havre	03/06/1916	04/06/1916
War Diary	Lillers	05/06/1916	05/06/1916
War Diary	S Hilaire Cottes	06/06/1916	12/06/1916
War Diary	Houchin	13/06/1915	13/06/1915
War Diary	N. Maroc	14/06/1916	18/06/1916
War Diary	Houchin	19/06/1916	20/06/1916
War Diary	N. Maroc	21/06/1916	23/06/1916
War Diary	Houchin	24/06/1916	24/06/1916
War Diary	Divion 36 b I 24	25/06/1916	30/06/1916
War Diary	Divion	01/07/1916	02/07/1916
War Diary	Maisnil-Les-Ruitz	03/07/1916	03/07/1916
War Diary	Calonne	04/07/1916	10/07/1916
War Diary	Bully-Grenay	11/07/1916	17/07/1916
War Diary	Calonne	15/07/1916	22/07/1916
War Diary	N.E. Maroc	23/07/1916	30/07/1916
Miscellaneous	Raid on Enemy Trenches Night Of 18/19th July 1916 Extracts from 119th Inf. Bde. O.O. No 8	17/07/1916	17/07/1916
Map			
War Diary	S. Maroc	30/07/1916	10/08/1916
War Diary	Bully Grenay	11/08/1916	13/08/1916
War Diary	Calonne	14/08/1916	16/08/1916
War Diary	Les Brebis	17/08/1916	23/08/1916
War Diary	Loos	24/08/1916	01/09/1916
War Diary	N.E. Maroc	02/09/1916	06/09/1916
War Diary	Loos	07/09/1916	11/09/1916
War Diary	Les Brebis	12/09/1916	19/09/1916
War Diary	N. Maroc	20/09/1916	23/09/1916
War Diary	S. Maroc	24/09/1916	30/09/1916
War Diary	Maroc	01/10/1916	11/10/1916
War Diary	Loos	12/10/1916	29/10/1916
War Diary	Les Brebis	30/10/1916	31/10/1916
Miscellaneous	Ref. Para 6. Operation Orders No. 1 Appendix 4	19/10/1915	19/10/1915
Miscellaneous	Appendix War Diary Oct. 1916		
War Diary	Magnicourt	01/11/1916	01/11/1916
War Diary	Foufflin-Ricametz	02/11/1916	03/11/1916
War Diary	Fortel	04/11/1916	04/11/1916
War Diary	Le Meillard	05/11/1916	15/11/1916
War Diary	Rougefay	16/11/1916	16/11/1916
War Diary	Bonnieres	17/11/1916	17/11/1916
War Diary	Le Souich	18/11/1916	21/11/1916
War Diary	Gezaincourt	22/11/1916	22/11/1916
War Diary	St Ouen	23/11/1916	23/11/1916
War Diary	Eaucourt Sur Somme	24/11/1916	30/11/1916
Miscellaneous	Ref. Para. 6. of Operation Order No. 1 Of 13.10.18	18/10/1918	18/10/1918
Miscellaneous	A Co		
Miscellaneous	Headquarters. 119th Infantry Brigade.	01/01/1917	01/01/1917
War Diary	Eaucourt Sur Somme	01/12/1916	10/12/1916
War Diary	No 12 Camp Les Celestine	11/12/1916	16/12/1916

War Diary	No 13 Camp	17/12/1916	18/12/1916
War Diary	No 13 Camp Les Celestine	19/12/1916	25/12/1916
War Diary	Camp 17 Suzanne	26/12/1916	31/12/1916
War Diary	Rancourt Sector	01/01/1917	04/01/1917
War Diary	Camp 17	05/01/1917	08/01/1917
War Diary	Asquith Flats	09/01/1917	12/01/1917
War Diary	Bouchavesnes Sector	13/01/1917	16/01/1917
War Diary	Asquith Flats	17/01/1917	18/01/1917
War Diary	Camp 17	19/01/1917	22/01/1917
War Diary	Rancourt Sector	23/01/1917	25/01/1917
War Diary	Maurepas Ravine	26/01/1917	27/01/1917
War Diary	Camp 12	28/01/1917	10/02/1917
War Diary	Suzanne	11/02/1917	11/02/1917
War Diary	Rancourt	12/02/1917	15/02/1917
War Diary	Albany Support Area	16/02/1917	19/02/1917
War Diary	Rancourt	20/02/1917	22/02/1917
War Diary	Camp 21	23/02/1917	24/02/1917
War Diary	Bray	25/02/1917	08/03/1917
War Diary	Suzanne	09/03/1917	09/03/1917
War Diary	Frise	10/03/1917	12/03/1917
War Diary	Clery Sector	13/03/1917	15/03/1917
War Diary	Curlu	16/03/1917	20/03/1917
War Diary	Feuillacourt	21/03/1917	21/03/1917
War Diary	Driencourt	22/03/1917	25/03/1917
War Diary	Bouchavesnes	26/03/1917	06/04/1917
War Diary	Bouchavesnes and Etricourt	07/04/1917	09/04/1917
War Diary	Etricourt	10/04/1917	17/04/1917
War Diary	Dessart Wood Nr Fins	18/04/1917	18/04/1917
War Diary	Dessart Wood	19/04/1917	21/04/1917
War Diary	Gouzeaucourt	22/04/1917	26/04/1917
War Diary	S.W. of La Vacquerie	27/04/1917	30/04/1917
War Diary	Dessart Wood	01/05/1917	05/05/1917
War Diary	Battn in Bde Reserve	05/05/1917	06/05/1917
War Diary	Front Line	07/05/1917	14/05/1917
War Diary	Dessart Wood	15/05/1917	23/05/1917
War Diary	Equancourt	24/05/1917	30/05/1917
War Diary	Sorel Le Grand	31/05/1917	04/06/1917
War Diary	Villers-Plouich (Front Line)	05/06/1917	13/06/1917
War Diary	Gouzeaucourt	14/06/1917	21/06/1917
War Diary	Sorel Le Grand	22/06/1917	28/06/1917
War Diary	Gonnelieu (Front Line)	28/06/1917	30/06/1917
War Diary	Gonnelieu Sector Front Line	01/07/1917	06/07/1917
War Diary	Gouzeaucourt	07/07/1917	09/07/1917
War Diary	Gouzeaucourt Reserve Bullets	10/07/1917	12/07/1917
War Diary	Gonnelieu	13/07/1917	19/07/1917
War Diary	Gonnelieu Rt Sub-Sector	20/07/1917	21/07/1917
War Diary	Gouzeaucourt	22/07/1917	27/07/1917
Heading	War Diary 18th (S) Bn The Welsh Regt. August 1917		
War Diary	Gouzeaucourt	28/08/1917	29/08/1917
War Diary	Gonnelieu	30/08/1917	31/08/1917
War Diary	Gonnelieu	01/08/1917	02/08/1917
War Diary	Grantham	03/08/1917	03/08/1917
War Diary	Villers Plouich	04/08/1917	07/08/1917
War Diary	Grantham Supports Terrace	08/08/1917	15/08/1917
War Diary	Villers Plouich Pinesight	16/08/1917	20/08/1917
War Diary	Villers Plouich Pinesight Suffers Trenches	23/08/1917	29/08/1917

War Diary	Gouzeaucourt Trescourt Rd	30/08/1917	31/08/1917
Heading	War Diary 18th. (S) Bn. The Welsh Regiment September 1917		
War Diary	Villers-Plouich	01/09/1917	08/09/1917
War Diary	Gouzeaucourt	09/09/1917	16/09/1917
War Diary	Villers-Plouich	17/09/1917	24/09/1917
War Diary	Gouzeaucourt	25/09/1917	30/09/1917
Heading	War Diary 18th (S) Bn. The Welsh Regt October 1917		
War Diary	Gouzeaucourt	01/10/1917	07/10/1917
War Diary	Railton	08/10/1917	08/10/1917
War Diary	Peronne	09/10/1917	10/10/1917
War Diary	Gouy-En-Artois	11/10/1917	29/10/1917
War Diary	Lucheux	30/10/1917	31/10/1917
Heading	War Diary 18th (S) Bn. The Welsh Regiment November 1917		
Heading	War Diary. Intelligence Summary 18th (S) Batt. Welsh Regt. November 1917		
War Diary	Lucheux	01/11/1917	16/11/1917
War Diary	Gouy-En-Artois	17/11/1917	17/11/1917
War Diary	Gommiecourt	18/11/1917	19/11/1917
War Diary	Barastre	20/11/1917	21/11/1917
War Diary	Doignes	22/11/1917	22/11/1917
War Diary	Graincourt	23/11/1917	23/11/1917
War Diary	Anneux Chapelle	24/11/1917	25/11/1917
War Diary	Havrincourt	26/11/1917	26/11/1917
War Diary	Lechelle	27/11/1917	27/11/1917
War Diary	Berles au Bois	28/11/1917	30/11/1917
Heading	War Diary 18th. (S) Bn. The Welsh Regiment. Dec 1917		
War Diary	Berles-Au-Bois	01/12/1917	02/12/1917
War Diary	Ervillers	03/12/1917	04/12/1917
War Diary	Durrow Camp Mory	05/12/1917	08/12/1917
War Diary	Left Subsector Right Brigade	09/10/1917	14/12/1917
War Diary	Railway Reserve	15/12/1917	20/12/1917
War Diary	Croisilles	21/12/1917	30/12/1917
Heading	War Diary 18th Bn Welsh Regt. January 1918		
War Diary	North Camp Mory	01/01/1918	01/01/1918
War Diary	In The Field	02/01/1917	05/01/1917
War Diary	In Support Railway Reserve	06/01/1918	08/01/1918
War Diary	Railway Reserve	09/01/1918	09/01/1918
War Diary	Left Subsector Left Brigade.	10/01/1918	14/01/1918
War Diary	North Camp Mory	15/01/1918	17/01/1918
War Diary	Stray Support Left Sub Sector Left Brigade	18/01/1918	20/01/1918
War Diary	Stray Support	21/01/1918	21/01/1918
War Diary	Railway Reserve Brigade Support	23/01/1918	25/01/1918
War Diary	Stray Support Left Sub Sector Left Brigade	26/01/1918	27/01/1918
War Diary	Left Sub Sector Left Brigade	28/01/1918	28/01/1918
War Diary	Stray Support Left Sub Sector Left Brigade	29/01/1918	29/01/1918
War Diary	North Camp Mory	30/01/1918	31/01/1918
Heading	War Diary February 1918 18th Welsh Regt.		
War Diary	North Camp Mory	01/02/1918	02/02/1918
War Diary	Stray Support Left Subsector Brigade.	03/02/1918	04/02/1918
War Diary	Stray Support	05/02/1918	07/02/1918
War Diary	Railway Reserve	08/02/1918	10/02/1918
War Diary	Durham Camp No 2.	11/02/1918	19/02/1918
War Diary	Durham Camp	20/02/1918	21/02/1918

War Diary	No 2 Camp Blairville	22/02/1918	24/02/1918
War Diary	Blairville Camp	25/02/1918	27/02/1918
War Diary	No 2 Camp Blairville	28/02/1918	28/02/1918
Heading	18th Battalion The Welsh Regiment March 1918		
Heading	18th Welsh Regt War Diary For March 1918		
War Diary	Gouy-En Artois	01/03/1918	03/03/1918
War Diary	No 2. Camp Blairville	04/03/1918	12/03/1918
War Diary	Northumberland Lines Mercatel	13/03/1918	22/03/1918
War Diary	In The Field	22/03/1918	22/03/1918
War Diary	Cross Roads North Of Judas Farm	23/03/1918	27/03/1918
War Diary	Sombrin	28/03/1918	29/03/1918
War Diary	Dieval	30/03/1918	31/03/1918
Heading	18th Battalion The Welsh Regiment April 1918		
Heading	War Diary April 1918		
War Diary	Dieval	01/04/1918	01/04/1918
War Diary	Rue Montigne	02/04/1918	02/04/1918
War Diary	Estaires	03/04/1918	05/04/1918
War Diary	Estaires & Fleurbaix Sector	06/04/1918	15/04/1918
War Diary	Moulle	16/04/1918	21/04/1918
War Diary	Zudausques	22/04/1918	29/04/1918
War Diary	Momelin (Bois Du Ham)	30/04/1918	30/04/1918
Miscellaneous	18th Battn The Welsh Regt.	16/04/1918	16/04/1918
Heading	18th (S) Bn The Welsh Regiment. War Diary Volume No. 24 May 1918		
Heading	War Diary May 1918		
War Diary	St Momelin (Bois-du-Ham)	01/05/1918	01/05/1918
War Diary	Terdeghem	02/05/1918	02/05/1918
War Diary	Bois-Du-Ham	03/05/1918	10/05/1918
War Diary	Staple (Herodrome) P.25.c.7.7.	11/05/1918	15/05/1918
War Diary	Staple O.30.a.22.	16/05/1918	31/05/1918
Heading	War Diary For 1/18th June 1918		
War Diary	Staple	01/06/1918	09/06/1918
War Diary	Stuyver N.17.b.00.10	10/06/1918	14/06/1918
War Diary	St Momelin (Bois-du-Ham)	15/06/1918	17/06/1918

washroom/2

40TH DIVISION
119TH INFY BDE

18TH BN WELSH REGT
JUN 1916-JUN 1918.

FROM UK

To 16 BN 47 BDE

WAR DIARY or INTELLIGENCE SUMMARY

Army Form C. 2118

(Erase heading not required.)

Instructions regarding War Diaries and Intelligence Summaries are contained in F. S. Regs., Part II. and the Staff Manual respectively. Title Pages will be prepared in manuscript.

ORDERLY ROOM 0 -8 JUN 1916

18 Welsh Regt

Map Ref: FRANCE 1: 40,000

Place	Date	Hour	Summary of Events and Information	Remarks and references to Appendices
HAVRE	3.6.16	7.00	Main body of Battalion disembarked from Connaught & King Edward & marched to No 1 Rest Camp. Transport detail & SS "Argus" Bound. Arrived at Rest Camp 11.15	
	4.6.16	7.30	Batt" (less "C" Coy) marched out & entrained at GARE DU MARCHANDISE. Halts at MONTREUIL, BUCHY & ABBEVILLE. Remainder of Batt" entrained at GARE DU MARITIME at 19.AM	
LILLERS	5.6.16	6.30	Detrained at LILLERS & marched to billets at S. HILAIRE COTTES arriving in billets at 8.00. Second trainload arrived at 17.00	
S.HILAIRE COTTES	6.6.16		Batt" in rest	
	7.6.16		Coy Parades	
	8.6.16			
	9.6.16			
	10.6.16		2nd Lt H.C. Stacey sick & removed to hospital	
	11.6.16		1 L.D.Ame shot trying to return reg.	
	12.6.16			
	13.6.16	7.00	Left S.HILAIRE COTTES & marched to HOUCHIN via LILLERS & ALLOUAGNE. Encamped	
HOUCHIN				
N.MAROC	14.6.15	10.00	Marched to N.MAROC. Received French instruction with 1st BDE (K15 SHEET 36B) VIA NOEUX-LES-MINES & LES BREBIS	
	15.6.16		Trench instruction { A & B Coys to 10th GLOUCESTERS C & D Coys to 1st CAMERONS	
	16.6.16		"	
	17.6.16		" 3 wounded	
			1 killed 1 D.I.W. 4 wounded	
			1 killed, 1 bomber died, 2 wounded	
			28932 Sgt Bacon D. Coy shot at & killed by enemy sniper { Total casualties Officers - O.R. 1b
	18.6.16	13.00	Marched to HOUCHIN via LES BREBIS - MAZINGARBE - MINGE - Encamped	
HOUCHIN	19.6.16		Batt" in rest. 1 Accidentally wounded - 1 backing shortening to accident	
	20.6.16		Batt" in rest	
N.MAROC	21.6.16	9.00	Batt" moved to Trenches A. B Coys, and 2nd Royal Sussex C & D Coys to 2nd K.R.R. Casualties - NIL	
	22.6.16		Batt" in Trenches. Casualties - Officers - Nil, O.R 2 killed 4 wounded (1 sick)	

Army Form C. 2118

WAR DIARY or INTELLIGENCE SUMMARY

(Erase heading not required.)

Ref. FRANCE

II

Instructions regarding War Diaries and Intelligence Summaries are contained in F.S. Regs., Part II. and the Staff Manual respectively. Title Pages will be prepared in manuscript.

Place	Date	Hour	Summary of Events and Information	Remarks and references to Appendices
N. MAROC	23.6.16	—	Battⁿ in Trenches. Casualties — 1 O.R. wounded	
HOUCHIN	24.6.16	3.00	Battⁿ marched from trenches via LES BREBIS & NOEUX-LES-MINES to camp at HOUCHIN — Casualties 1 wounded	
DIVION 36 I 24	25.6.16	10.00	Battⁿ marched via BRUAY to DIVION (36th Division) Billet Area at DIVION — Casualties 1 O.R. sick	
"	26.6.16	—	2 sick — 1 Casualty reported for duty.	
"	27.6.16	—	1 sick reported for duty	Battⁿ in rest.
"	28.6.16	—	1 sick	
"	29.6.16	—	2 sick	
"	30.6.16	—		

ORDERLY ROOM
No ....
30 JUN. 1916
18TH (SER.) BATTALION.
THE WELSH REGIMENT (GLAM.)

R. Grant Thorold
Lt. Col.
Cmdg 18th Bn. The Welsh R.

WAR DIARY
or
INTELLIGENCE SUMMARY

(Erase heading not required.)

Army Form C. 2118

40/ July

July 1916 Vol 2

ORDERLY ROOM
No ....
-0 JUL 1916
18TH (SER.) BATTALION.
THE WELSH REGIMENT (GLAM.)

HEADQUARTERS
31 JUL 1916
40th DIVISION

J.C.
8 sheets

Place	Date	Hour	Summary of Events and Information	Remarks and references to Appendices
DIVION	1.7.16		Bathe in rest	
"	2.7.16		" – 1 accidental injury, 1 wounded, 1 transf.	
MAGNIL-LES-RUITZ	3.7.16		Left DIVION for MAGNIL-LES-RUITZ near BRUAY 1 acc. wnd. 1 sick	
CALONNE	4.7.16		Left MAGNIL-LES-RUITZ for relieved MOLOGRANE 2nd R.Bks at CALONNE in support – 7 sick	
"	5.7.16		In support – 2 sick 2 wnd.	
"	6.7.16		" – Casualties NIL	
"	7.7.16		Relieved 12th S.W.B. in line, 4.Bn. R.Bdz – 1 wnd. 1 sick 1 rept. for duty	
"	8.7.16		In line – 2 wnd. 1 sick 1 rept. for duty	
"	9.7.16		" 1 d.of.wnds 1 wnd.	
"	10.7.16		" 1 wnd 1 sick 1 transferred	
BULLY-GRENAY	11.7.16		Relieved by 12th S.W.B. Bn. moved to BULLY-GRENAY as bath. in Bde. reserve – 1 sick	
"	12.7.16		1 sick 2 rept. to duty	
"	13.7.16		1 rept. to duty	
"	14.7.16		Casualties NIL	
CALONNE	15.7.16		Relieved 12 S.W.B. Co 4. Bn. R.Bde. Casualties nil. In line. Casualties Nil.	
"	16.7.16		" R/Lt Lawrence bagged sniper – Casualties 1 killed, 1 wnd, 1 sick	
"	17.7.16		" "Raid on enemy trench by 13W m. Attacked accept. 1 sick, 1 transf.	
"	18.7.16		To support at CALONNE interned Murph by 1st 1st R.W.B. 2nd /27. O.Salzburg wnd 2 D.R. missing believed killed, 1 wnd, missing 2 wnd	

Army Form C. 2118

WAR DIARY
or
INTELLIGENCE SUMMARY
(Erase heading not required.)

Instructions regarding War Diaries and Intelligence Summaries are contained in F. S. Regs., Part II. and the Staff Manual respectively. Title Pages will be prepared in manuscript.

ORDERLY ROOM
- 0 JUL. 1916
18TH (SER.) BATTALION.
THE WELSH REGIMENT (GLAM.)

Place	Date	Hour	Summary of Events and Information	Remarks and references to Appendices
CALONNE	20.7.16		In support. 1 wnd	
"	21.7.16		" 1 gassed (by mine) 2 sick, 1 Kanifer	
"	22.7.16		" " 1 sick	
N.E. MAROC	23.7.16		Relieved at CALONNE by 19th H.L.I. 12th Bde. Bn. relieved 12th Suffolks at N.E. MAROC in reserve to 120th Bde Canadian MR	
" "	24.7.16		In reserve. 2nd Lts. L.J. SHARKEY & E.B. Percival joined from 20th Warwick R. reporting. 1 sick	
" "	25.7.16		" " Casualties. NIL	
" "	26.7.16		" " 1 sick	
" "	27.7.16		" " 1 reported Duty & transferred to base	
" "	28.7.16		" " 2nd Lt. G.H. Young joined from 20th Warwick R. 2 sick	
" "	29.7.16		" " Casualties. NIL	
" "	30.7.16		Afternoon Relieved mutually with 19th A.N.S.H. in L. Subsector, CAZONNE	

Raid on Enemy Trenches:
night of 18/19th July 1916

Extracts from 119th Inf. Bde. O.O. No 8 17.7.16

Objects I To obtain identification
         II "   "   prisoners
         III To damage enemy's defensive system

PHASES   I   Artillery fire on hostile wire
         II Patrols
         III Further Artillery fire
         IV Raid on hostile trenches

~~Report~~

PHASE I Wire to be cut during the day on both sides of enemy sap at M 15 d 3.8 5.7.

BARRAGES a (ZERO at 12.15 a.m.)

(a) M.20 b. 20.00 to M.20 b. 67.50
    DUMMY BARRAGE by Howitzers
    commencing at ZERO for 15 mins.

(b) M 15 d 35.20 to M.15 d. 42.82
    commencing at ZERO & finishing by arrangement between O.C. 18th Welch & O.C. R. Group Artillery

II BARRAGES
(Continued) (c) Artillery fire on Mg d 8.2

(d) Artillery fire & trench mortar fire on enemy trenches (2nd line) at CITE DES CORNAILLES

PHASE II Two patrols on night of 17/18th reconnoitred ground and from this and other sources a sketch map was drawn.

PHASE III was not necessary

PHASE IV RAID

Orders issued to 2nd Lt O. Salisbury & 2nd Lt R.D Grosscart by O.C. 18th Welch R.

"The Artillery Barrage will commence at 12.15 a.m. & by this time you must be up to the gap in the wire. Immediately the barrage begins you will rush to your positions, 2nd Lt Salisbury with 3 Bayonet men & 4 bombers enter the gap at point to clear trench up to point "A""

"Simultaneously 3 Bayonet men enter at point G & work down to B also 1 N.C.O & 4 bombers keep on parapet & work from G to B"

III

"Remaining 3 men at G & follow others to B. Three of the six men at B will work a little way down towards C and three towards H"

2nd Lt R.D. Grossart's party.

"3 Bayonet men and 3 Bombers will rush across trench at E & move on to D where the 3 Bayonet men enter trench & look out, one up & one down the trench with the other standing between them. The 3 Bombers will remain on the parapet above the Bayonet men who will themselves carry bombs"

"Two Bayonet men enter trench at point E & two bombers one on each side of the trench will remain on the parapet. Three Bayonet men with bombs will enter trench at E & work towards H meeting 2/Lt Salisbury's party when they will work more down trench towards D"

"Yellow ribbons (distinguishing badges) will be removed & pay books & any letters or papers handed in"

"Wire "footballs" will be taken for blocking trench"

"Telephone will be run out to gaps

IV as soon as dark."

"1 N.C.O' & 5 Scouts will move out at dark & will carefully watch the gaps & report any movement there to the telephone operator"

"The main party will move at 23.30

"C. Coy will furnish a covering party on the right of 1 N.C.O. & 8 men who will move out with the scouts"

V. Report by O.C. 18th Welch R.

'I regret the failure of the operation, due, I consider, to the following cause

(a) The moon was bright & so it was impossible to actually cut through wire before the attack; so strands of wire left by artillery delayed some of the parties.

(b) We encountered a strong working party of Germans who were evidently assembled there to mend their wires & though we had taken out 144 bombs these were exhausted & 2/Lt Groves anti' party had to retire from want of ammunition when he had dead & wounded Germans in the pit in front of him.

(c) Lt Salisbury being wounded left his party without a leader. This was a great misfortune.

(d) The finding of German Trench running out in front of Gap left out by our Artillery on left created a certain confusion as it was not shown on our aeroplane photograph & the party who should have got to pt. C. did not get there as quickly as they should.

ORDERLY ROOM
No. ....
_ JUL. 1916
18TH (SER.) BATTALION,
THE WELSH REGIMENT (GLAM.)

WAR DIARY or INTELLIGENCE SUMMARY

Army Form C. 2118

18th Bn. Notts & Derby Regiment

Vol 3

Place	Date	Hour	Summary of Events and Information	Remarks and references to Appendices
S. MAROC	30.7.16		Front line. Quiet day – Casualties N/L	
"	1.8.16		" " Casualties 3 O.R. wounded	
"	2.8.16		" " 1 O.R. killed, 8 wounded – mainly aerial darts	
"	3.8.16		" " 3 O.R. wounded	
"	4.8.16		" " Quiet. Casualties N/L	
"	5.8.16		" " Enemy mine exploded on DOUBLE CRASSIER. Casualties 1 and 2 O.R. Battalion in local relief.	
"	6.8.16		" " 5 O.R. wounded 1 detached.	
"	7.8.16		" " 3 O.R. wd 3 sick 1 detached – quiet	
"	8.8.16		" " 2nd Lt. R.D. GROUART transferred to R.E.C. – 2 O.R. wnd	
"	9.8.16		" " 2 O.R. killed 3 wnd.	
"	10.8.16		" " Relieved by 19th A.I.F. 10 O.R. wnd.	
BULLY GRENAY	11.8.16		Bn. in reserve. 2 O.R. sick	
"	12.8.16		" Lt. PALEWIS sick 1 O.R. and 1 sick.	
"	13.8.16		Relieved 12 Sw. B. in CALONNE Sept Grassier.	
CALONNE	14.8.16		Enemy active. 4 O.R. killed 5 wnd. 2nd Lt. W.M. Rees wounded severely 1 sick	
"	15.8.16		1 O.R. killed 5 wnd 1 detached. Lt. D.B. DAVIES + 2nd Lt. J. CORBETT to BETHUNE 1/5 R.F.C.	
"	16.8.16		Relieved by 19th KRR. 2 O.R. wnd	
LES BREBIS	17.8.16		1 sick	
"	18.8.16		1 wnd	
"	19.8.16		BDE in reserve 3 sick	
"	20.8.16		1 killed	
"	21.8.16			
"	22.8.16		2 sick	
"	23.8.16			
"	24.8.16		Relieved 6 R.I.F. in support. 1 wnd	
"	25.8.16		" " 3 sick	
"	26.8.16		" " 1 sick	
"	27.8.16		2/Lt O.B. RIDOUT evacuated sick. 1 O.R. back	
LOOS	28.8.16		Relieved 12 S.W.B. in front line. 1 Dg. to A wnd	
"	29.8.16		Quiet	
"	30.8.16		Quiet, 1 O.B. wnd.	
"	31.8.16		" 1 casualty	

H.W.H.

WAR DIARY or INTELLIGENCE SUMMARY

Army Form C. 2118

Vol 4

Place	Date	Hour	Summary of Events and Information	Remarks and references to Appendices
LOOS NEMAROC	1/9/16		Front Line. Batt. relieved mutually with 12th S.W.B. in trenches in N. Maroc. Casualties NIL	
"	2/9/16		In Reserve. Lt. P.A. Lewis returned to duty	
"	3/9/16		" Casualties Nil. 2 O.R. reported sick. One transferred to base	
"	4/9/16		" Casualties Nil. 1 O.R. rejoined	
"	5/9/16		" 2 O.R. sick	
LOOS	6/9/16		Front line. Relieved 12th S.W.B. in LOOS Right Sub-Sector, handing trench over to 17th WELSH. 3 O.R. sick. 1 dead	
"	7/9/16		" 1 killed 2 wounded	
"	8/9/16		" 1 wounded	
"	9/9/16		" 2 wounded, 2 transferred to Divisn. underage	
"	10/9/16		" 2nd Lieut. H.C. Stacey slightly wounded, 7 O.R. wounded, 1 killed	
"	11/9/16		" Batt. relieved mutually with 12 S.W.B. at Les Brebis. 5 sick	
LES BREBIS	12/9/16		BDE in Reserve. 2nd Lt. R.F.W. Rees, w.t.d. arriv. J.S.G. Hackney reported for duty from No. 6 I.B.D.	
"	13/9/16		" Casualties Nil. 5 O.R. transferred to next camp	
"	14/9/16		" 1 sick. Capt. S.B. Davies reported returned to duty	
"	15/9/16		" Casualties Nil. 4 O.R. reported for duty	
"	16/9/16		" 1 sick. Major J. McAdam awarded M.M. for act of gallantry on the 10th inst.	
"	17/9/16		" 1 Sick.	
"	18/9/16		" Batt. relieved mutually with 14 A.V.S.H. at N. Maroc. Casualties Nil	
N. MAROC	19/9/16		In Support. Sgt. E.C. Beacon & 2nd Sgt. G.D. Williams awarded D.C.M. for acts of gallantry on 8th & 9th inst	Appendices I
"	20/9/16		" Casualties Nil.	Divisional Orders attached
"	21/9/16		"	
"	22/9/16		Batt relieved mutually with 19th R.W.F. and went into reserve at S. Maroc	
S. MAROC	23/9/16		Bn in Reserve. Casualties 1 O.R. wounded	
"	24/9/16		" 2nd Lt. I. Bowen reported for duty. Batt. received draft of 2 N.C.O.'s and 28 men	
"	25/9/16		"	
"	26/9/16		" Batt in MAROC LEFT SUBSECTOR. Casualties - Nil.	
"	27/9/16		Front line. Relieved 12th S.W.B. in MAROC LEFT SUBSECTOR. Casualties 5 O.R. wounded	
"	28/9/16		" Snipers very active from Craissier and scored several hits. Casualties Nil. Including 4 by premature burst	
"	29/9/16		" Very Quiet. 1 O.R. wounded	
"	30/9/16		" Casualties Nil.	

Edward Thos Rufford
Cmdg. 15th Welch

WAR DIARY or INTELLIGENCE SUMMARY

Army Form C. 2118

Place	Date	Hour	Summary of Events and Information	Remarks and references to Appendices
MAROC	1st	1916	3o Bde left Estrades MAROC. Raid on enemy trenches to obtain identifications. Enemy ovtres & his trenches was held by us for 45 minutes. Retaliation identification secured by helmet marked R.202.	
"			CASUALTIES 2ND LT E.A.K. ROBINSON } wounded 9 O.R. wounded	
"			2ND LT F. WYNNE JONES } 1 missing	
"			Sgt. W.Divine awarded Military Medal for gallantry on the occasion of this raid	
"	2nd		LINE 10.'R.arrived.	
"	3rd		" 1.O.R.wnd /sick	
"	4th		To SUPPORT. material relief with 12TH S.W.B. MAJOR H.R. WOOD assumes 2nd in command vice MAJOR S.W.TROT appointed to 1st Corps. Casualties 1.O.R.wnd 3 sick	
"	5th		SUPPORT Casualties 1.O.R.wnd 3 sick	
"	6th		" " 4.O.R.sick	
"	7th		" " 2.O.R.sick	
"	8th		" " 3.O.R sick	
"	9th		" " 3.O.R killed 1 wnd (Bellis) killed with Sgr.G.2 knives). Draft 1 N.C.O. 32 men	
"	10th		" " 4.O.R.sick	
"	11th		" " NIL	
LOOS	12th		To LINE R.Subsector LOOS (late L.MAROC) Casualties NIL	
"	13th		CASUALTIES NIL	
"	14th		" " 1.O.R.wnd	
"	15th		" " 1.O.R wnd	
"	16th		" " 2.O.R.Kngd 1 sick	

WAR DIARY or INTELLIGENCE SUMMARY

Army Form C. 2118

PAGE V

Place	Date	Hour	Summary of Events and Information	Remarks and references to Appendices
LOOS	Oct 17th	19/6	LINE Heavy trench mortar & rifle grenade barrage from DOUBLE CRASSIER.	
"	18th		Casualties 1 O.R. killed 5 wounded	
"	19th		" 2 O.R. killed 3 wounded 2 sick	
"	20th	To	" 1 O.R. sick	
	21st		SUPPORT Mutual relief with 17th Bn R. Carmathew	
	22nd		" CAPT. E.B. DAVIES sick & O.R. sick	
	23rd		" 1 O.R. sick	
	24th		" NIL	
	25th		" CAPT. R. BOWLES sick	
	26th		RESERVE M.MAROC Casualties NIL	
	27th		" " 1 O.R. killed	
	28th		" " NIL	
	29th		" " NIL	
			" Relieved by 13th Middx 74th Bde 24 Div.	
LE1 BREBIS	30th		REST Casualties NIL	
	31st		40th Div. moves into G.H.Q. Reserve.	

Rhu Thurlblow Lt Col
Cmdg 10th Bn The Welch Regt

Appendix 4

After Order.

Ref. Para 6. Operation Orders No 1. of 18.10.18

Attached replica of tracing shows objectives with Blue, Red, & Green Lines.

A. & B. Coys will take 1st objective (Blue Line) as already detailed & C. & D. Coys will similarly pass through them & proceed to 2nd objective (Red Line) where they will halt from Zero plus 74 mins to Zero plus 116 mins, whilst halted on Red Line C & D Coys will commence consolidating, but will move on with barrage at Zero plus 116 mins, & A & B Coys will move up & complete the digging in on Red Line. If necessary when C & D Coys arrive in Green Line, B Coy will move up & occupy left of Green Line. If this is done A Coy 15 WELSH will move up & take their place in support line as already detailed.

R R Davies
2/Lt & actg adjt
14th Battn Welsh Regt

19/10/18.

To Brigade

Appendix. War Diary Oct. 1915

The battalion has now occupied the sectors round Loos for nearly 5 months and a short resumé is given below:-

CASUALTIES   There have been about 279 casualties of which 110 either remained at duty or have since returned leaving at present a permanent loss of 169. Casualties to officers have been few, no officer having been wounded in our trenches by enemy fire. Of the 9 officer casualties, 3 were wounded on raids, 1 in 'No Man's Land' (very slightly), 1 accidentally in our line & 4 were sick.

WORK   Constant work has been done on the trenches & they have been greatly improved, both for safety & comfort though latterly, holding an extended front with very few men, it has been impossible to maintain the trenches as at first. Many shelters have been erected and dug-outs built.

RAIDS   Two more important and 3 minor raids have been made or attempted mainly to secure identification. The first raid accounted for about 30 of the enemy, in another case enemy trenches were empty, in another identification was secured & in the last the enemy evacuated his sap & disappeared behind his wire into 'No Man's Land' & could not be found in the dark. The enemy has once attempted to raid our trenches, but was driven off with no casualties on our side.

PATROLS - WIRING   No Man's Land has been patrolled every night when the battalion has been in the line. Sgt. Lawrence & his 'Maconochie' gang have done excellent wiring & considerably strengthened its defences.

SPECIALISTS SNIPERS had a singularly successful period shooting S. from the NORTHERN CRASSIER bagging 60 Huns at the rate of about 3 a day.
OBSERVATION has been good & many enemy positions marked down.
BOMBERS have periodically raided enemy trenches & latterly have held the DOUBLE CRASSIER.

CRIME has been almost absent only 2 serious cases having been tried by F.G.C.M.

DECORATIONS 2 D.C.M's & 2 Military Medals have been awarded to N.C.O's & men of the Battalion.

R Grant Thorold Lt Col
Cmdg 18th Bn. The Welch Regt.

WAR DIARY
or
INTELLIGENCE SUMMARY

(Erase heading not required.)

Army Form C. 2118

Instructions regarding War Diaries and Intelligence Summaries are contained in F.S. Regs., Part II. and the Staff Manual respectively. Title Pages will be prepared in manuscript.

1 8 Welsh Regt Vol 6

Place	Date Nov. 1916	Hour	Summary of Events and Information	Remarks and references to Appendices
MAGNICOURT	1st		28189 Llewellyn J. Proceeded to Base Depot Rouen being under 18½ years of age. Authority MS AW 110A of 1/11/16 119 Bde B/283/G.L. of 2/11/16	
FOUFFLIN-RICAMETZ	2nd		1 Sick. March. 7 km SE St Pol.	
"	3rd		1 Sick. 1 Classified P.B.	
FORTEL	4th		March. Draft 1 Offr 38 men arrived	
LE MEILLARD	5th		March.	
"	6th		Capt W. Newton 2/Lt W.R. Petty sick. Capt Richards C Coy leaves for 1st Army School. Lt McWilliams takes command C. Coy. 2/Lt T. Phillips appointed Sig Offr. 1 OR to 1st Army School. (Offrs servant)	
"	7th		Pte Jones J.B. (24.10.16) rejoined unit 7/11. Lt Carne O. 27737 rejoined from No. 2 Training Camp Etaples	
"	8th		Training as per programme Casualties Nil	
"	9th		" " " " "	
"	10th		" " " (Battalion Drill) "	
"	11th		" " " " "	
"	12th		Church Parade. 2 Sick.	
"	13th		Training as per programme	
"	14th		" " " " 2 Sick. 1 evacuated (under age)	
"	15th		March to ROUGEFAY (11 miles) 1 evacuated (under age) Officers 3 ORs 129 leave in motor buses as carrying party	
ROUGEFAY	16th		Training as per programme. 1 Offr 79 OR leave as carrying party. 2 Sick	

C.E. G.W. Dawson Capt 18 Welsh 2 sheets

Army Form C. 2118

WAR DIARY
or
INTELLIGENCE SUMMARY
(Erase heading not required.)

Instructions regarding War Diaries and Intelligence Summaries are contained in F. S. Regs., Part II. and the Staff Manual respectively. Title Pages will be prepared in manuscript.

Place	Date November 1916	Hour	Summary of Events and Information	Remarks and references to Appendices
BONNIERES	17th		March from ROUGEFAY. 5 miles. 2 Officers go on leave (Capt G Jones B Co. Lt Coe D Coy)	
LE SOUICH	18th		March 9 miles. 3 Officers go on leave (Major Wood & Lawrence. Capt Ebbs. OR 2 rejoined from hospital	
"	19		Church Parade 10am - 11am. 1 - 3.30 pm resumption training. 1 OR on leave (R.S.M.)	
"	20		Training On leave 1 OR. 2nd Lt Jones joins unit. Posted temporarily to C. Co.	
"	21		Training (as per programme) 1 OR on leave	
GEZAINCOURT	22		March from LE SOUICH. (8 miles) 1 to Base Depot. Auth. HQM Div. 1408. 1 OR on leave	
"	23		" GEZAINCOURT (14 miles) 1 OR on leave	
ST OUEN	24		" ST OUEN (14 miles) 1 OR on leave	
EAUCOURT SUR SOMME	25		Training 2 Offrs on leave, 1 OR. 2 sick	
"	26		" as per programme. On leave 1 Warrant Offr. 2/Lt Turnbull joins unit 4 Offrs & 207 OR rejoin unit from 5th Corps H.A.	
"	27		" " " 1 Sick	
"	28		" " " On leave Col Thorold	
"	29		Route march	
"	30		Training as per programme	

GW Edward Capt
18th Welsh

Order

Ref: Para 6 of Operation Orders No 1 of 13.10.18

Barrage The Barrage will lift after 4 minutes & thereafter move on at the rate of 100 yds per 4 mins except that it will halt beyond 1st objective from Zero plus 24 mins to Zero plus 34 mins.

FORMATION During the advance to 1st objective B Coy will detail one Rifle Section to mop up right edge of Ravine on R. yet. as far as 1st objective to act as flank guard as barrage will not traverse the Ravine as already detailed.
From 1st to 2nd objective C. Coy will act to take measure to A. Coy

REMARKS

On arrival at final objective Coy. will if situation permits push patrols forward to the general line West end of FOREST to RICHEMONT.

R R Davies

18.10.18

A 6

Headquarters
119th Infantry Brigade.

In accordance with instructions herewith "War Diary" for Dec. 1916.

Field
1/1/17

R Grant Thorold Lieut. Col.
Cmdg 18th (S) Batt.
The Welch Regt.

WAR DIARY or INTELLIGENCE SUMMARY

Army Form C. 2118

Place	Date 1916	Hour	Summary of Events and Information	Remarks and references to Appendices
EAUCOURT sur SOMME	Dec 1.		Training as per programme. Casualties nil. 1 OR rejoined unit	
"	2		" " " " " Afterspanshown Casualties nil	
"	3		Church Parade. Casualties nil	
"	4		Training as per prog. " 1 Offr sick (to No 2 Stationary Hospital) 1 OR retd from 119th TMB	
"	5		" " " " " 1 OR "	
"	6		" " " " " 1 OR sick 2 Offrs 1 OR granted leave	
"	7		" " " " " NIL	
"	8		" " " " " 5 OR sick	
"	9		" " " " " 1 Offr " (to No 2 Stationary Hospital) 1 OR sick	
"	10		Entrained at PONT REMY STN. Detrained at EDGE HILL STN Nr BUIRE SUR ANCRE. Hence marched to LES CELESTINE CAMP 12. Casualties 1 OR sick	
No 12 CAMP LES CELESTINE	11		Pioneer work CASUALTIES SICK 1 OR	
"	12		" SIGNAL SECTION inspected by G.O.C. CASUALTIES NIL	
"	13		" " " CASUALTIES 1 OR SICK	
"	14		" " " " NIL	
"	15		" " " 2 OR transferred to Base Depot 1 Sick	
"	16		Evacuated from No 12 to No 13 Camp, 1 mile distant NE	
No 13 CAMP	17		Pioneer work CASUALTIES NIL	
"	18		" " " 1 OR sick	

Capt Thos M WPC
Cmg 15th (S) Batt
Duke of Wellt Regt

WAR DIARY
or
INTELLIGENCE SUMMARY

(Erase heading not required.)

Army Form C. 2118

Place	Date	Hour	Summary of Events and Information	Remarks and references to Appendices
No 13 CAMP LES CELESTINS	Dec	19	Pioneer work nil	
"		20	5 OR rept. at from No 6 IBD Depot. Major Supple rejoins CASUALTIES NIL	
"		21	" Casualties NIL	
"		22	" C.O. + 2/M to MAUREPAS. Reconnaissance of new sector. CASUALTIES 2 sick	
"		23	" CASUALTIES 2 sick	
"		24	" "	
"		25	" "	
		26	March. CASUALTIES SICK 1 Offr.	
CAMP 17 SUZANNE		27	To Support Battalion Area near LE FOREST CASUALTIES Wounded 3 Offrs 1 OR	
		28	In Support CASUALTIES Nil	
		29	" " Killed 1 OR Wounded 8 OR Caused by shell striking French ammunition dump	
		30	" " Relieved 12th SWB 7.30 pm CASUALTIES 5 OR sick	
		31	From Support to front line. 1 OR struck off strength clerk to 1st Corps MGO Authy sgmd 1st Corps 23-12-16 1 OR rejoins unit	

Signed [illegible] Lt/Col
Comdg 16th (S) Batt.
The Welsh Regt.

WAR DIARY
or
INTELLIGENCE SUMMARY

Army Form C. 2118

18 Welsh Regt
Vol 8

Place	Date 1917	Hour	Summary of Events and Information	Remarks and references to Appendices
RANCOURT SECTOR	Jan 1		In the line. Casualties Wounded OR 2. Rejoined from hospital 1 OR	
"	2		" " "	
"	3		" " Sick 7 OR	
"	4		" " Wounded 2 Col. R Grand Thorold Sick 3 OR	
CAMP 17	5		Relieved by 13 East Surrey Regt. Battn. relief 9.30pm marched to MAUREPAS. Hence by Motor Lorries to Camp 17. SUZANNE. Casualties Killed 1 OR Wounded 3 OR Sick 2 OR	
"	6		Rejoined Unit 2 OR	
"	7		Major Murphy assumes temp. Command of Battn. Casualties NIL	
"	8		Major Wood returned from Hosp. & takes over command from Major Murphy. Casualties Sick 1 OR	
"	9		Capt Rathgate RAMC to ALBERT 4 days Sanitation Course. Casualties Sick 4 OR	
BOUCHAVESNES ASQUITH FLATS	10		To Support Batt. Area Right Pde BOUCHAVESNES SECTOR. Relief 1.40pm	
"	11		In support. Casualties Sick 2 OR	
"	12		" " 2 OR	
"	13		" " 2 OR	
BOUCHAVESNES SECTOR	14		Relieved 12th SWB BOUCHAVESNES SECTOR Casualties NIL 1 OR rejoined unit	
"	15		In the line. Casualties. Sick 3 OR	
"	16		" " 3 OR	
"	17		" " 4 OR	
ASQUITH FLATS	17		Relieved by 12th SWB - Retd to SUPPORT AREA ASQUITH FLATS. Casualties. Sick 2 Offrs In support. Casualties Sick 2 OR	

Army Form C. 2118

WAR DIARY
or
INTELLIGENCE SUMMARY
(Erase heading not required.)

Instructions regarding War Diaries and Intelligence Summaries are contained in F.S. Regs., Part II. and the Staff Manual respectively. Title Pages will be prepared in manuscript.

Place	Date	Hour	Summary of Events and Information	Remarks and references to Appendices
ASQUITH FLATS	18 Aug		In support. CASUALTIES SICK 5 OR. Rejoined from IBD 1NCO 3 OR	
CAMP 17	19		To Camp 17. SUZANNE. CASUALTIES SICK 1 OR	
"	20		Casualties SICK 2 OR	
"	21		" " 2 OR. 2 Officers joined Unit	
"	22		In the line RANCOURT SECTOR. CASUALTIES SICK 9 OR	
RANCOURT SECTOR	23		In the line. CASUALTIES SICK 5 OR. 2/Lt G. Benson reported for duty	
"	24		" " " 2 OR	
"	25		Relieved by 13 SWB. Went to Reserve MAUREPAS RAVINE. Casualties SICK 1 OR. WDD 1 OR	
MAUREPAS RAVINE	26		In reserve CASUALTIES SICK 9 OR	
"	27		To Camp 12 " " 2 OR	
CAMP 12	28		Training. Nil. 2/Lt F.S.G. Chappell appointed Adjt. Reported for duty 2/Lt F. Pascoe. Rejoined Unit 2 Off. 2 OR	
"	29		Training. Boche aeroplane bombing activity.	
"	30		" CASUALTIES SICK 1 OR	
"	31		" SICK 1 Off. 1 OR. 1 OR rejoined Unit	

Hugh N Woods Lieut Col
Comdg 15 (S) Batt.
The Welch Regt.

1875 Wt. W593/826 1,000,000 4/15 J.B.C. & A. A.D.S.S./Forms/C. 2118.

Army Form C. 2118

WAR DIARY
or
INTELLIGENCE SUMMARY
(Erase heading not required.)

Instructions regarding War Diaries and Intelligence Summaries are contained in F.S. Regs., Part II. and the Staff Manual respectively. Title Pages will be prepared in manuscript.

18 Welch Regt
Vol 9

9. E.
2 sheets

Place	Date 1917	Hour	Summary of Events and Information	Remarks and references to Appendices
CAMP 12	Feb 1		Training as per programme. CASUALTIES. NIL	
"	2		" " " " " "	
"	3		" " " " SICK 1 OR	
"	4		" " " " NIL. 1 OR reported for duty	
"	5		" " " " NIL	
"	6		" " " " NIL	
"	7		" " " " 1 OR to Base Depot under 19 yrs of age. Duty 1101(A) 4to Div	
"	8		" " " " 2 OR rejoined unit	
"	9		" " " " 1 OR sick. CO for reconnaissance of Sector	
"	10		Left Camp 12 for SUZANNE (Camp 17) CASUALTIES 1 OR to England (Cadet Battn)	
SUZANNE	11		Left Camp 17 for RANCOURT SECTOR. Relieved 12th R.I.R. CASUALTIES. 3 OR Sick	
RANCOURT	12		In the line. CASUALTIES. KILLED 1 OR WOUNDED 3 OR SICK 2 OR	
"	13		" " " " " 1 OR " 1 OR	
"	14		" " " SICK 2 OR	
"	15		" " Relieved by 12th S.W.B. To Support An Area ALBANY. CASUALTIES. SICK 15 FEB. 10 OR	
ALBANY SUPPORT AREA	16		In support CASUALTIES SICK 4 OR	
"	17		" " " " 4 OR	
"	18		" " " " 3 OR	
"	19		Left support area for the line. Relieved 12th SWB. 1 OR to Base under age. CASUALTIES SICK 3 OR	
RANCOURT	20		In the line. CASUALTIES SICK 1 OR	
"	21		" " " " 1044 3 OR. 3 Offrs reported for duty from No 6 I.B.D.	
"	22		" " Relieved by 2/1st Middx Regt. Marched to CAMP 31. CASUALTIES SICK 4 OR	

WAR DIARY
or
INTELLIGENCE SUMMARY

(Erase heading not required.)

Army Form C. 2118

Place	Date 1917	Hour	Summary of Events and Information	Remarks and references to Appendices
CAMP 21	Feb	23	CASUALTIES SICK 2 OR	
"		24	Marched to BRAY - took over Billets 14th A.S.H. CASUALTIES SICK 34 OR	
BRAY		25	CASUALTIES SICK 2 OR	
"		26	" " 6 OR	
"		27	" " 8 OR. 5 OR rejoined Unit.	
"		28	" " 1 OR.	

[signature]
Maj. A Wood L Col
Cmdg. 1/5 Batt.
Herts Regt.

WAR DIARY or INTELLIGENCE SUMMARY

Army Form C. 2118

(Erase heading not required.)

18 Welsh Regt

Vol 10

Place	Date	Hour	Summary of Events and Information	Remarks and references to Appendices
BRAY	Feb 1st		Work: Unloading trains & Quarry work. 2 Coys less 2 Platoons at LE PLATEAU unloading ammunition.	
"	" 2		CASUALTIES 1 sick	
"	" 3		do. do. do. CASUALTIES. 2 OR 2 sick	
"	" 4		do. do. do. " 2 "	
"	" 5		do. do. do. " NIL	
"	" 6		do. do. do. " 3 sick (1 to England)	
"	" 7		do. do. do. 1 NCO & 1 OR reported from No. 6 IBD. CASUALTIES NIL	
"	" 8		Left for Camp 19 SUZANNE at 4 p.m. CASUALTIES 9 OR	
SUZANNE	" 9		Left Camp 19 for Reserve Area. CLERY sector. CASUALTIES 3 OR	
FRISE	" 10		In reserve CASUALTIES SICK 1 OR. Relieved 2nd R.W.F. CASUALTIES. 1 OR	
"	" 11		" " NIL 1 Coy HOWITZER WOOD. 1 Coy OMNISCOURT	
"	" 12		Relieved 13th S.W.B. " 3 OR " 2 OR rejoined. 2 Officers reported for duty	
CLERY SECTOR	" 13		In the line " Killed 1 OR. Wounded 3 OR Sick 1 OR	
"	" 14		" " " SICK 10 R	
"	" 15		Relieved by 21st Middx Regt. Relief 13 p.m. Marched to CURLU CASUALTIES 6 OR	
CURLU	" 16		In reserve 1 OR rejoined from hospital. CASUALTIES NIL	
"	" 17		" " CASUALTIES NIL	
"	" 18		" " " "	
"	" 19		" " " SICK 8 OR	
"	" 20		Left for the line Relieved 11th KOR near FEUILLACOURT. CASUALTIES SICK 1 OR	

E.O.C.
2 Jul
106

Army Form C. 2118

WAR DIARY
or
INTELLIGENCE SUMMARY
(Erase heading not required.)

Instructions regarding War Diaries and Intelligence Summaries are contained in F.S. Regs., Part II. and the Staff Manual respectively. Title Pages will be prepared in manuscript.

Place	Date	Hour	Summary of Events and Information	Remarks and references to Appendices
FEUILLACOURT	Feb. 21		Marched to DRIENCOURT relieved 14th Q. 95. H. CASUALTIES Sick 2 OR	
DRIENCOURT	" 22		In the line. CASUALTIES. Nil.	
"	" 23		" " " " "	
"	" 24		" " " 1 OR Sick	
"	" 25		" " " 1 OR wounded, acc. Relieved by 1/4 Warwick Regt at 8 a.m. marched	
BOUCHAVESNES	" 26		to BOUCHAVESNES. Battalion on road repair work under supervision C.R.E. CASUALTIES. Nil.	
"	" 27		do " " " " 1 OR rejoined	
"	" 28		do CASUALTIES. Nil 1 OR reported from No 6 IBD	
"	" 29		do " " SICK 2 OR	
"	" 30		do " " " 2 OR	
"	" 31		do " " " 1 OR	

Jagl R Wood Lt Col
Comdg 18th (S) Batt Middx Regt

Vol XI
2. Albury
11 E
5 sheets

WAR DIARY / INTELLIGENCE SUMMARY

Army Form C. 2118

16th WELSH REGT

Place	Date	Hour	Summary of Events and Information	Remarks and references to Appendices
BOUCHAVESNES	1st / 2nd April 1917		Battalion at BOUCHAVESNES. Battalion paraded for bathing at CRANIERES. Production of A Coy by C.O. 6 p.m. Three hundred men employed on road mending on MOISLAINS - NURLU Road. C.O. proceeds to ETRICOURT to reconnoitre place of assembly, in event of an alarm. 2/Lt Rumsey & ten pioneers to ETRICOURT to take over billets. 2/Lt KNOPREES joined. Major Edward & Burghard to Senior Officers Course.	
"	3rd "		Batch of 300 men employed BOUCHAVESNES - MOISLAINS Road from 8.30 am to 4.30 pm. C.O. reconnoitres line to be held in support with Coy Commanders. Capt Withers fell from his horse & suffering from concussion and dislocated his arm. 2/Lt Howell joined from Cadet School (7th LEINSTERS) (CASUALTY 1 officer injured)	
"	4th "		Bath. employed as yesterday. Adjutant and all subaltern reconnoitred line of Resistance and performed tactical scheme at EQUANCOURT. CASUALTIES - 1 O.R. sick to England	
"	5th "		Bath. employed as yesterday. Instruction of C Coy by C.O.	
"	6th "		Last day prior to move. Tactical instruction to C.O. to all officers 11.30 to 1.30. 2/Lt Robinson & 5 men from Bde Lewis Gun School. 2/Lt Barnett & 7 men from Bde Bombing School. Both Returned to Leave 7 - 10th 2/Lts to B Coy. O.C.	
" and ETRICOURT	7th "		Marched from BOUCHAVESNES to ETRICOURT via MOISLAINS. Distance abt 6 miles. 15 T.M.B. handcart and 6 Lewis gun handcart were pulled by the battalion. Officers billets in Strang's house, men in tents, all horses accommodated in Stables. Sundry covers. Bath in Divisional Reserve employed on Road Making. A requires Batch to shew line of Resistance from N edge of FINS on a line running NNW for 1500 yards. 2/Lt Moring to wear the badges of Captain. CASUALTIES - 1 O.R. to hospital arm 3 O.R. to Divisional Salvage BOUCHAVESNES.	
"	8th "		2/Lts May and Slatter, to leave 10th - 19th. 300 men employed on road repair MANNANCOURT - MOISLAINS Road. C.O. and Coy commanders reconnoitred line of resistance from FINS to VASSE central Examination (written) for all Battalions.	
"	9th "		300 working on road mending as yesterday. A Coy bathed. Shakespeare Players & pierrots at football.	

Result August 1 -
1875 Wt. W593/826 1,000,000 4/15 J.B.C. & A. A.D.S.S./Forms/C. 2118.

WAR DIARY
INTELLIGENCE SUMMARY

18th WELSH REGT.

Army Form C. 2118

Place	Date 1917	Hour	Summary of Events and Information	Remarks and references to Appendices
ETRICOURT	10th April		Bn working on MANNANCOURT—MOISLAINS road relaying. 2/Lt Whaley L/Jones reported for duty ex Stock Div School. 2/Lt Pascoe & James to Infantry Course ETENHAM. B Coy bathed.	
"	11th		Rev Mr La Poste Payne C of E joined. Bn work on road as yesterday. C Coy bathed.	
"	12th		Bath played 14th Kings at football. Result Won 2-1.	
"	13th		Bath worked on road as yesterday. Ranks gone to leave 14+23. 50 R.+H.O. Lukes ork Bde Competition.	
"	14th		Bath works on road MOISLAINS—MANNANCOURT. Played 17th Welsh R in Bde football Competition. Result lost 9-0.	
"	15th	"	Bath worked as yesterday.	
"	16th	"	Bath inspected by G.O.C. and spent day rebuilding billets etc. Inspection unsatisfactory and another ordered for 17th. Worked at night digging Main Line of Resistance, pouring rain. Returned to billets 6am 17/4/17.	
"	17th	"	G.O.C. inspection cancelled. Bath relieved Bde Works in forward area and became Bde Sup. at 2/Lt Whaley released from Class arrest after interview with Brig Gen and to be leave for 12 months. Orders of March D.E.A.D. H.Q. Bath marched from ETRICOURT at 1.30 pm billet complete at 5 pm. QM Stores Transport remain at ETRICOURT. Bath in huts + canvas bivouacs. Captn Montgomery Jones rejoined ex Course in Command. Re Ranoves reported absent from line of march	
DESSART WOOD N¹ FINS	18th	"	Bn in Bde Support. Worked on line of resistance digging. B+C Coy from 6.30 pm to 10.30 pm H+D Coy 10.30 pm to 2.30 am. Day spent in improving bivouacs shelters. Sgt Webb to leave	

WAR DIARY

INTELLIGENCE SUMMARY

Army Form C. 2118

1st WELSH REGT

Place	Date	Hour	Summary of Events and Information	Remarks and references to Appendices
DESSART WOOD	19th April		Bn in Bde Support. Day spent in improving accommodation. Bns worked at night 6.30 – 10.35 p.m. digging line of resistance. Entrances investigated in Bn lines. C Coy & Hd Qtrs A Coy by 4th – Commanded to-day 19th and 20th 4th and Commanded to-day 19th inspected.	
			Reconnees attended at BIANANCOURT by Major.	
	20th	"	Lt Edmunds returned from leave. Bn received orders to take up position in advance line of resistance, holding a two battalion front A & C in right holding from R25d Central through Q30d8575 to junc of Stream with road Q30d5530. B & D from thence to make an assault on enemy outposts 19th RWF + 15th SWB respectively. The two latter battalions to make an assault on enemy outposts and relieve up at line running R26b55 – R20d00 – FIFTEEN RAVINE. Zero hour probably dawn (4:15am)	
	21st	"	At 4:15 a.m. our artillery opened a barrage on enemys outpost line. Fifteen minutes before this the 19th RWF and 15th SWB are in fighting platoon formation well outside our advanced line of Resistance and our battalion 1st Welsh are in support in the latter A & C Coy Commanded by Capt Fitch at the disposal of the CO. 19th RWF and B & D Coy Commanded by Capt Kyffin at the disposal of the CO. 15th SWB.	
			Capt Fitch is wounded at the outset of the attack by the enemy counter barrage. The (C) SWB catch when twenty of our B Coy men to mop up about twenty of the enemy who have hidden themselves in the attack and arriving into the trenches of the 15th SWB. The party under 2/Lt Williams SWB, arriving in rear of the offender prisoners, killing the remainder. The whole of the attack is successful, all objectives have been taken.	
			Our Casualties – Killed 2. Wounded 19. Capt Fitch wounded.	

Army Form C. 2118

WAR DIARY
or
INTELLIGENCE SUMMARY
(Erase heading not required.)

18TH WELSH REGT

Place	Date	Hour	Summary of Events and Information	Remarks and references to Appendices
GOUZEACOURT	22nd April 1917		18th Welsh relieved the 19th R.W.F. in the line taken on 21st at 2am. The Captured line running from (Map 57cNE) R20c 8000 – R20c 0050 and Ravine to Jn. of railway. Bn. H.Q. was attached S. of GOUZEACOURT at Q26 c 3030. Left & Right B.J. & A. C in Reserve. 2/Lt & 50 O.R. wounded through trans with Men. On O.R. wounded.	
	23rd		Batt. reviewed its position and received orders to attack position S.W. of LAVACQUERIE in 24th. The line to be taken by the Battn. was from R20 a 19 – R20 e 1045 – R20 e 5020. The 17th Welsh Regt were attacking on half. Zero was 4.15am with last half hrs orders to occupy high ground in rice savannahs there with eight feeling from before Zero. At 9.30 hr the 12 tanks were established at the Quarry R.19. A Cy (2/Lt Robinson) move forward & has occupied objective at 11.30am with 70 casualties. Covering party was pushed out while light hearted posts a line of trenches to be consolidated by the remainder of A Co. The German were bayonets by the enemy party. At 2.30am A Cy had orders the positions and were ready to support the advance of 17thWelsh. K. Curtis and the barrage was dropped and all objectives were gained. B Co. pushed forward two platoons to establish a line between A Cy & 17th Welsh. Two posts were made and 1/Lt. and 29 (twenty) casualties: 3 slightly wounded.	
"	24th "		Batt. had a front gained. Continue work of consolidation.	
"	25th "		Continue improving new line.	
"	26th "		A & B front line. D Support. C Reserve. 2/Lt Robinson & men went forward to engage hostile working party which advanced. Dugout searched and GRANATENWERFER complete with shot was captured. No casualties.	

Should read 24th

Army Form C. 2118

WAR DIARY
INTELLIGENCE SUMMARY
(Erase heading not required.)

18th WELSH REGT

Instructions regarding War Diaries and Intelligence Summaries are contained in F. S. Regs., Part II. and the Staff Manual respectively. Title Pages will be prepared in manuscript.

Place	Date	Hour	Summary of Events and Information	Remarks and references to Appendices
Souplu La VACQUERIE	27th April		Road our Battalion out that this C.o.B from this Dow that A reserve. 2d Platoon + C men took mobile charge + blew up both dugout reinforcement. formed last night. Casualties Nil.	
"	28th		Capt Moran joined from leave. Casualties Nil.	
"	29th		Lt McCrophter to leave. Lieut Swift Jellicoe in in front line were wire more like Support taking over from 14th RWF in FIFTEEN RAVINE. Casualties 10R killed by sniper.	
"	30th		The 20th Middlesex delivered in FIFTEEN RAVINE and we move into Brigade Reserve in DESSART WOOD. Casualties Nil.	

Hugh R Wood Lt Col
Comdg 18th Welsh Regt

1875 W: W593/826 1,000,000 4/15 J.B.C. & A. A.D.S.S./Forms/C. 2118.

Army Form C. 2118

WAR DIARY or INTELLIGENCE SUMMARY

18th Welsh Regt

(Erase heading not required.)

Place	Date	Hour	Summary of Events and Information	Remarks and references to Appendices
DESSART WOOD	1/5/17		BATTALION employed in cleaning up & refitting. 2/Lieut G. & J.O.R. to Brady Camp ETINEHEM. 2/O.R. to Corps School, 2/Lieut H.L. Obed & 11 O.R. to Gen Course XVth Corps.	
	2/5/17		The whole Battalion bather at ERICOURT.	
			Lieut. Conyers proceeded on leave. 4th – 14th May 1917.	
	3/5/17		O.R. to hospital.	
			O.C. and Company Commanders reconnoitred the line in case of future operations. Lieut. Dr. Mackie and Lieut. C.F. Percival rejoined from 14 Army School Flexicourt. The following officers joined the Battalion from Etre and were posted as follows:– Lieut. J.H. Curtis "C" Coy, 2/ Lt W.S. Prevost "D" Coy, Lieut. E.S. Jenkins "C" Coy. 1 O.R. from 6 Entf/ R/I Sch/B.	
	4/5/17		Battalion continued cleaning & refitting.	
			The Runners tried by T.O.C.R. for selection.	
			3/Lieuts Hargreaves Lewis, Evans, J. Taylor & Hern Wms 1 O.R. to hospital. 1 O.R. from 6 Entf/ Base Schd.	
	5/5/17		Battalion moved from desert camp to Battalion in Brigade Reserve. Brigade in Relief in YPRACOURIE. Battalion with H.Q. Headqrs. Co. Company at R.29.C and 3 Companies in shelter trenches at R.29.d. (Map 57c.SE) O.C. took up his position at R.29.b.94 with an advanced H.Q. in Quarry K.29 & Chaplain & Band in Quarry K.2.C.Central (?) in the event of H/W Battalion being called on, the C.O. & 2nd in Comd. & the C.Q. in Quarry.	12.C [?] sheet

WAR DIARY
or
INTELLIGENCE SUMMARY

(Erase heading not required.)

Army Form C. 2118

Instructions regarding War Diaries and Intelligence Summaries are contained in F. S. Regs., Part II. and the Staff Manual respectively. Title Pages will be prepared in manuscript.

Place	Date	Hour	Summary of Events and Information	Remarks and references to Appendices
Bath in Bill Row (Con)	5/5/17		The Barrage is ordered at 11pm, but withdrawn later	
	6/5/17		The raid continued and drawn at 1am. The Brigade on left was driven in right not held at end. Our Brigade reached their objective village several casualties on the enemy returned with some casualties. Both Cmdrs. N.b. Both returns to DESSART WOOD at 4 am. Relieved 12th South Wales Borderers in English and 20 Bn. in position by 10.30 pm. Dispos. line X.31.c. R.20.f. R.W.A. 2.O.R. & Bde Adml & H.Q.S.	
Front line	7th		Artillery activity Nil. Commenced taking up our hooks, much system of trenches. Bivouacs & trench dumps under supervision of R.E. Casualties: 2.O.R.W. & Pierce to Le Cure LE TOURQUET. 1 O.R. to D.R. on leave.	
	8th		Situation quiet. Patrols report no enemy seen. Major R. Willis M.C. transferred to Reserve Assembled & Command the Battalion. 1 O.R. on leave to leave	

WAR DIARY or INTELLIGENCE SUMMARY

Army Form C. 2118

(Erase heading not required.)

Place	Date	Hour	Summary of Events and Information	Remarks and references to Appendices
Bout luck	9th		Situation generally quiet. Casualties 1 O.R. wounded. 3 O.Rs to hospital. 10th (W. Yorks) and 3 O.Rs to 1st Corps Sig. Co. v RT & 2/ Durhams & 7 O.R. to 4th Army School.	
"	10th		Situation Quiet. Reconnoitering patrol under 2/ Lieut Gittoes brought back + Review from "Le Bercels", a position held by the enemy. Casualties 1 O.R.D. 2 O.R. from gas: over 3 O.Rs.	
"	11th		Hostile artillery activity. Casualties 8 O.Rs wounded. 1st Battalion to the Rubis.	
"	12th		On the R.R. shelled intermittently. Much aerial activity. Casualties 5 O.R. Returns to duty from hospital 3 O.R. to hospital 2/ Lieuts & 11 O.R. to Bde Bomb School, 1/O.R. to conduct George Croston "2/ Rotterick & 7 O.R. to Bde LG School. 2/ Markham & 1 O.R. from Bde Sigel &c.	
"	13th		Situation quiet. At night a patrol went out under 2/ Lieut at 10pm 2/Lt Brook, Dunlop, 2 O.R. Broad & Information. 1 O.R. to hospital and information.	

1875 Wt. W593/826 1,000,000 4/15 J.B.C. & A. A.D.S.S./Forms/C. 2118.

Army Form C. 2118

WAR DIARY
or
INTELLIGENCE SUMMARY

(Erase heading not required.)

Instructions regarding War Diaries and Intelligence Summaries are contained in F. S. Regs., Part II. and the Staff Manual respectively. Title Pages will be prepared in manuscript.

Place	Date	Hour	Summary of Events and Information	Remarks and references to Appendices
Bon line	14/5/17		Situation generally quiet. Some aerial activity. Battalion moved to DESSART WOOD in Brigade Reserve. Coy. HQ one proceeded to Etables as instructors to Reinforcements. Revd PM Richbaw joined from leave.	
DESSART WOOD	15th		Relief completed at 3 am. Bn Tailor's clerk to hospital. 2/Lts Curtis & Jex LG Course XV Corps Sch. 2/Lt Butler XV Corps Bombing course. 1 OR Bombing course XV Corps Sch.	
"	16th		Commenced Battalion training. Companies employed by Commandg cleaning billeting. 3 OR to hospital. 2 OR from hospital. 2/Lt Jenkins & 3 OR rejoined from leave. Bombing School as instructors.	
"	17th		Battalion training continued. 3 OR inoculated. LG class of 12 per company commenced under 2 Lt Lewis. 11 ORs joined from 6 Infy Base Dept. 4 OR to hospital. The Officer (Lt Kenyon) & 5 OR to PT Course Equancourt. 2 OR to Bde School.	
"	18th		Battalion training continues. 3 OR from hospital. 2 OR to hospital.	
"	19th		Battalion training continues	

WAR DIARY
or
INTELLIGENCE SUMMARY
(Erase heading not required.)

Army Form C. 2118

Place	Date	Hour	Summary of Events and Information	Remarks and references to Appendices
DESSART WOOD.	19th		Battalion training continued. H. Sergeant & I.O.R to Hospital	
	20th	10 A.M	C of E. Divine Service held at 10 A.M.	
		10 A.M	Nonconformists service " 10 A.M	
		9 P.M	Roman Catholic " " 9 P.M.	
		11.15 P.M	W. inspection of Battalion by C.O. at 11.15 A.M.	
		2 P.M.	Inspection of M.Gun equipment by C.O. at 2 P.M.	
			I.O.R. to Field Ambulance 7 INS.	
	21st.		Battalion bathed at EQUANCOURT and carried on Battalion training. Lieut S.T. Lawrence & 1 M.R. Proctor to Transport Camp at 6 Brille 100 men inoculated.	
	22nd		Battalion went into Brigade support - hard over work from 12th South Wales Borderers. A Coy were employed in digging intermediate line and Quarries at Q.35.c.0.3. & B Coy were employed on tunnelling Quarries at Q.29.t.12 Bathr HQ C and D Coys at DESSART WOOD. I.O.R to Hospital I.O.R to UK on leave. I.O.R to Pigeon course.	

WAR DIARY
or
INTELLIGENCE SUMMARY

(Erase heading not required.)

Army Form C. 2118

Place	Date	Hour	Summary of Events and Information	Remarks and references to Appendices
BERTH	23rd		Left BESSART WOOD for EQUANCOURT. BATTALION in SUPPORT. A & B Coy bivouacing in the open. C & D Company continuing training. 1 Offr to Roerive (Lt. Edmunds) 1 OR & UK on leave. 20 R-drivers + 3 OR to Pt. Course Equancourt.	
EQUANCOURT	24th		Training continued with C & D Coys. A & B Coys working on Tunnelling and Intermediate line respectively. 1 OR to Kashna. 1 OR from hospital. 2 OR from Gas Course. 1 OR to UK on leave.	
"	25th		Training continued C & D Coys. A & B Coys employed as on 24th inst. 1 OR to Kashna. 1 OR to UK on leave. 2 OR from Pigeon Course.	
"	26th		Brigade in Divisional reserve. 1 NCO & 16 men attached R.E. FINS. A & B Coys returning Battalion at EQUANCOURT. C & D Coys mobilies D Coy. Camp D Companies billets at FINS. 2 OR to UK on leave.	

WAR DIARY
or
INTELLIGENCE SUMMARY
(Erase heading not required.)

Army Form C. 2118

Place	Date	Hour	Summary of Events and Information	Remarks and references to Appendices
ERVANCOURT	27th		C of E Divine Service at 10·30 a.m. Non conformists at 9 a.m. Roman Catholic at 10 a.m. All Coys dine 30 Lewis ceremonial drill after church parade 2 pm to 5 pm A & B Coy Bathes. 21 O.R to Musketry Course Pont-Remy. 1 O.R to leave.	
"	28th		6 Officers and 200 O.R. to Dessart Wood for digging in former area made up of B, C & D Coys & part of H.Q. Capt. Young in charge of detachment. 1 O.R. from hospital. 1 O.R. to leave. J.O.R from hospital	
"	29th		Classes continue in [Gun + Bombing Company] continues work from Dessart Wood. 2: WB Roderick & 6 O.R. from Bde L. Gun school 2 Officers & 10 O.R from Bde Bombing school.	
"	30th		Bath. H.Q. A Coy & details marched to COREL LE GRAND and pitches camp on Southern side of village. 2/ Lt E.A.R.Robinson & 3 O.R. returned from Physical Training Course Equancourt. Maj O.T.R. Wood from leave.	

WAR DIARY or INTELLIGENCE SUMMARY

Army Form C. 2118

Place	Date	Hour	Summary of Events and Information	Remarks and references to Appendices
SOREL LE GRAND	2/5/-		Contains continued work from BESSART WOOD. Classes of instruction continues. Lieut. E.A.N. Robinson, Lieut. E.S. Jenkins and 7 O.R. to XVA Corps School of Instruction. Lieut. Reece, Lieut. Reed & Curtis & 7 O.R. returnes from Divt Corps School. 1 N.C.O. & 30 men rejoined from R.E. Base. 1 O.R. rejoined from Divising School Bernden.	

2/5/1917

Hugh Rwood Major for Lt Col
Commdg 11th Welsh Regt

WAR DIARY
or
INTELLIGENCE SUMMARY.
(Erase heading not required.)

Army Form C. 2118.

18th Welsh Regt — Vol 13

Place	Date	Hour	Summary of Events and Information	Remarks and references to Appendices
Sorel le Grand	1917 April 1st		The Artillery Bombardment delivered at present Went on during the most part in the Bryon line and System in rear near GOUZEAUCOURT. A lecture by CRA to all officers of the Brigade on LIAISON between RFA and Infantry. CO Brigade to tank and detachment at DESSART Wood.	
			Arrivals 2nd Lt. R. T Jones and 4 ORs reinforcements from Base 2nd Lt R=W Reed Joined at XV Corps School Russia 2nd Lt WM Mogol and 40 ORs reinforcements Allery This Regt Reed Orders to relieve from Brigade Reserve 1 OR returned from BOUCHON as trade.	
			Absences: 2 ORs to United Kingdom on leave	
	2nd		Companies continued work on the Trenches (Broom line) and Gates Battalion Class of instruction at SOREL continues CO inspected N.C.O.s and Men attached to 231 Field Coy. RE (works Bath) under command of Lt. M². Col. CO and 2nd in command inspected the front line to be taken over by the Battalion – Regl Aid station – VILLERS–PLOUICH 10 OR from Leave. 1 OR from Hospital. 1 OR from L.G. Course at Estaples	13 C
			Arrivals	

Army Form C. 2118.

WAR DIARY
or
INTELLIGENCE SUMMARY.
(Erase heading not required.)

Instructions regarding War Diaries and Intelligence Summaries are contained in F. S. Regs. Part II. and the Staff Manual respectively. Title pages will be prepared in manuscript.

Place	Date	Hour	Summary of Events and Information	Remarks and references to Appendices
Fort de Grand	1917 June 30		General Preparation for Relief. Relieved 13th Batt Yorkshire Regt in front line - Left entrance - MILLERS-TOVICH. Relief commenced 9.30 pm Completed 1 AM 4th June. "D" right Coy. "C" Left Coy. "A" right Support Coy. "B" left support Coy. Ree 25.95 Ree 80.60 (57 C 1E Znero) (Znero) Adventure 2 OR to Hospital	
	4th		On the front line trenches: At 2 am a red rocket signal observed 1030 up from Enemy lines and immediately an intense Barrage opened onto Right (D) Coy front line. The Enemy evening intended rushing no mans land, but were promptly turn hearted near entanglements. No mans Land, but were promptly attacked by our Patrol. The latter apparently fell back on our front trench. The bombardment was intense for about 20 minutes. Casualties: 2nd Lt R Mead (2nd in Command) wounded on the Eye (sh) + his Left 2 Lt W M Mead wounded. (see ½½½) Land (sh) + his left. OR. 1 OR killed. 1 OR died of wounds. 3 OR wounded-Hospital 6 OR slightly wounded but refined to duty. Departures: 1 OR to Hospital Ree. 81. Arrivals: 5 J OR Reinforcement from No 6 IBD. (15 had already served with the Batt)	

Army Form C. 2118.

WAR DIARY
or
INTELLIGENCE SUMMARY.
(Erase heading not required.)

Instructions regarding War Diaries and Intelligence Summaries are contained in F. S. Regs., Part II. and the Staff Manual respectively. Title pages will be prepared in manuscript.

Place	Date	Hour	Summary of Events and Information	Remarks and references to Appendices
VILLERS-PLOUICH (Front Line)	1917 June 5		Considerable work done on front line - digging new trench to connect posts on left way from Massey avenue - improvements never noticeable front. Emergency telephone wire laid to Right trench via Coy H.Q. from Battn. H.Q. 17th Oxford & Bucks Light Infantry Company moved to trenches near West of VILLERS PLOUICH - R.13.a.7.4. 730,210. Arrivals: 1 O.R. Hospital 1 O.R. rejoined from Brigade H.Q. Departure: 1 O.R. Hospital 2 O.R. Leave to United Kingdom	
	6		Battalion in front line trenches - VILLERS PLOUICH.	1 O.R. Killed 5 O.R. Wounded
	7		Internal Relief. "A" Coy relieve "D" Coy in right line {R.14.d.2.7. {R.8.c.6.5. "B" " "C" " on left of line {R.8.c.58.25 {R.7.d.4.6	
	8		In the line. Situation quiet - Enemy shells the village of VILLERS PLOUICH at intervals. Considerable work done on the line - cutting new trench to connect three advanced posts in order to advance front line about 300 yds	
	9		In the line	

WAR DIARY or INTELLIGENCE SUMMARY

Place: VILLERS PLOUICH (Front Line)

Date	Hour	Summary of Events and Information
1917 June 10		Normal situation on the front line trenches.
11		The Battalion was relieved by 1/5th Oxf & Bucks Regiment. Completed — A, B and D Coys took up accommodation in No. 18 Ravine R19 c 3.4 — 57c SE 1/20,000. C Coy and Batt Headquarters at Sunken Road Q 30 & 7.*. near G.9. GOUZEAUCOURT. Major M. Kennedy M.C. of the 18th H.L.I. (Machine Gun Company) attached to the Battalion to take Command whilst Lieut J.E. Hobbs is on leave.
12		Battalion in Support. The Battalion found all available men to the front line to complete the work of digging communication trench and place wire entanglements across front during the night.
13		In Support — usual work on the front line — R.E. Tape. Lieut J.E. Hobbs M.C. 9th Battalion Newton. Leave to the United Kingdom and Major M. Kennedy M.C. took over Temporary Command.

Army Form C. 2118.

WAR DIARY
or
INTELLIGENCE SUMMARY.
(Erase heading not required.)

Instructions regarding War Diaries and Intelligence Summaries are contained in F.S. Regs., Part II. and the Staff Manual respectively. Title pages will be prepared in manuscript.

Place	Date	Hour	Summary of Events and Information	Remarks and references to Appendices
GOUZEAUCOURT	1917 June 14		Battalion in support - and supplied working parties for the front line during the night. Enemy considerably more active with his Machine Guns on the working parties.	
	15		Battalion in support.	
	16			
	17		Battalion in support	
	18			
	19		The Battalion was relieved by the 1st Batt D. & S.H. 100hrs Bgde. and moved into Divisional Reserve. Battalion proceeded to bivouac on N.W. outskirts of the Village of SOREL-LE-GRAND vacated by the 1st R.D. & S.H. The men were tucked. Spent the day in cleaning up their Equipment.	
	20		Battalion went in for Training by Companies: Physical Jerking Bayonet fighting Lewis Drill Musketry Wiring	
	21		During the afternoon - Recreation. Lecture to the Officers and Senior N.C.O.'s by Lt Col. Kennedy - "Command"	

WAR DIARY
or
INTELLIGENCE SUMMARY
(Erase heading not required.)

Army Form C. 2118

Place	Date	Hour	Summary of Events and Information	Remarks and references to Appendices
SOREL Le GRAND	1917 June 22 23 24		Battalion in training. Recreational training for the Brigade Sports during the afternoon. Battalion in training.	
	25		Lt Col. S.R. Kerlie returned from leave and resumed command of the Battalion. Major W. Kennedy remains with the Battalion as second-in-Command.	
	26		Battalion carried out a practice attack in conjunction with the other Units of the Brigade; and with hostile aeroplanes. Lieut F.M. MATHIAS assumed the duties of adjutant. Capt. J.N. GILBEY departed for leave. Battalion in training. During the afternoon the Brigade Sports were held at DESCARD WOOD.	
	27		Battalion preparing equipment for trenches. The C.O. presented the following men with MEDAL RIBBONS:- 28580 Corpl NEWMAN, M. D.C.M. 2nd Lieut Private MORGAN, D. MILITARY MEDAL do JACKSON, W. Certificate for gallant conduct	

Place	Date	Hour	Summary of Events and Information	Remarks and references to Appendices
SOREL LE GRAND	June 27		The Battalion moved out of the Camp at SOREL-LE-GRAND the night of the 27th inst. and relief the 13th Yorks. Regt. in the Right Subsection of the MONCHELIEU Sector. R34a.0.7. to R27a.4.7 and R27d.4.7 to GOUZEAUCOURT - LE PAVE ROAD (inclusive). Two Companies in the front line and two in support at R33a.1.6 and R26d.8.2. Battalion Headquarters at R26d.7.8.	
	28		Battalion in the front line trenches: Work proceeded on completing wire in front of advanced posts and digging trench to connect posts. Also Communication trenches from Front line to rear Advanced line. Enemy attempted a raid on an Advance Trenches during the night with a party of 7 or 8. They were driven off and one Explosed two prisoners - both of whom were wounded - a Sergt. Major and Lance Corporal of the 123rd Grenadiers. The former died	

WAR DIARY
or
INTELLIGENCE SUMMARY

(Erase heading not required.)

Army Form C. 2118

Place	Date	Hour	Summary of Events and Information	Remarks and references to Appendices
GONNELIEU (Trenches)	1917 June 28		of wounds.	
	29		Battalion in the line. The enemy attempted a raid on the left Battalion, supported by heavy bombardment, but were repulsed.	
	30		Battalion in the line. Went went on the advanced line and were at 1.30 during the night. The enemy commenced an intense bombardment on the front of the Battalion on our right, and on our right Company front front. A little later an S.O.S rocket signal was fired by the right Battalion. The enemy were attempting a raid on the right of our front line and was replied with several casualties: the left Battalion captured two prisoners and brought in two dead Germans.	

J.O.Owen
Lt Col
Cmdg 18 Welsh

Army Form C. 2118

18 Welch Rgt

146
5 sheets

WAR DIARY or INTELLIGENCE SUMMARY
(Erase heading not required.)

Place	Date	Hour	Summary of Events and Information	Remarks and references to Appendices
GONNELIEU Sector —Front Line	1917 July 1		Battalion in the Line. Continued with the work of digging and deepening new French connecting advanced trench and placing more wire in front of position — thickening existing wire in front of new advanced line.	
	2		Battalion in the line	
	3		Battalion in the line. The Battalion front was extended to the right to Meadows Post (whereas R34A.77), taking over from the 2nd Middlesex Regiment. Battalion Boundaries after re-adjustment were: R33.b.66. Right Company H.Q at R33.b.66. Battalion Boundary R34a.5.3½. to GIN AVENUE R27a.8.5 to R34a.5.3½.	
	4		Battalion in line. A raiding party of 1 Officer and 19 O.R. proceeded and from Right Company front. The enemy wire at R28a.3½.2 approx. was blown up by a Bangalore Torpedo. Party encountered a second line of wire + were unable to effect an entry into enemy trench. Enemy engaged with bombs. 1 Officer Casualty. A second raiding party of 10 Officers and 20 O.R. went out from left Company to effect an entry at R22.a.2½.6. but were detected by the enemy and subjected to heavy rifle and M.G. fire. The party returned without incurring any casualties.	

WAR DIARY or INTELLIGENCE SUMMARY

Army Form C. 2118

Place	Date	Hour	Summary of Events and Information	Remarks and references to Appendices
GONNELIEU SECTOR Front Line	July 1917 5		Battalion in the Line. The Battalion was relieved on the night of the 5th inst by the 17th Batt. WELSH REGT. Relief completed at 12.45 A.M. on night 5th/6th July.	
	6		Battalion in Reserve. On completion of relief the Battalion moved into BRIGADE RESERVE as follows:- "A" Company at R.31.d.1.4. - QUENTIN MILL - Green Line - "B" do at X.1.b.15.80. "C" do at W.6.d.8.1. (Sunken Road) "D" do at R.31.d.1.4. Battalion Headquarters at W.6.d.0.2. (Sunken Road)	Ref 57D 20,000 GONNELIEU
GOUZEAUCOURT	7		Battalion in Reserve: Musketry etc: All Companies moved back night to work at Excavating NEW FRONT LINE Trench GONNELIEU SECTOR - Right Subsector. 119th Infantry Brigade Headquarters close at W.9.a.8.7. and then at GUILFORD - R.31.c.8.7 at 9.30 p.m. Battalion in Reserve.	
	8		Battalion in Reserve: Lieut Colonel. J.R Hicks reported sick	

WAR DIARY
or
INTELLIGENCE SUMMARY
(Erase heading not required.)

Army Form C. 2118

Place	Date	Hour	Summary of Events and Information	Remarks and references to Appendices
GOUZEAUCOURT Reserve Billets	1917 July 10.		Battalion in Reserve. Capt Gilbey evacuated to F.A. (Sick)	
"	11		" " "	
"	12		" " "	
GONNELIEU	13		Battalion in the line. Relieved 17th Welsh Regt in Right Sub sector. B.H.Q. R26.d.6.7. 2 Companies in front line 2 Coys in support. Patrols from 2 Coys (strength 10ff 200R ea) reached no man's land. No hostile patrols encountered	
"	14		Battalion in the line. Enemy artillery active during the day. At 9.15 p.m 3 red lights in succession sent up from enemy line. Nothing happened	
"	15		Battalion in the line.	
"	16		" " " At 10.30 p.m enemy opened intense TM bombardment near NEWTON POST [R34 a 9.8] At 12 midnight bombardment was repeated. Our artillery replied on both occasions.	
"	17		Battalion in the line. Capt Dowding 11th KORLR attached to Unit as 2nd in command. Inter Coy relief. B. Coy in support relieve C. Coy in right front. A Coy in support relieve D Coy on left front. Patrols thoroughly searched No Mans Land, but did not encounter any enemy patrols. Considerable hostile aerial activity during the day.	
"	18		Battalion in the line. 2nd Lt J.F. James off leave. Our sniper claims hit at R.28 c.8.3.	
"	19		" " " Enemy artillery fairly quiet. Capt Gilbey (attached) reports to unit. Several enemy aeroplanes flew over our lines, but were driven off by MG, A.A. fire.	

WAR DIARY
or
INTELLIGENCE SUMMARY

(Erase heading not required.)

Army Form C. 2118

Instructions regarding War Diaries and Intelligence Summaries are contained in F. S. Regs., Part II. and the Staff Manual respectively. Title Pages will be prepared in manuscript.

Place	Date	Hour	Summary of Events and Information	Remarks and references to Appendices
GONNELIEU Rt Sub-Sector	20/7/17		Battalion in the line. Capt Gilbey (attached) reports to duty.	Enemy artillery active
"	21st		The village shelled between 11.15am & 12.45am	
			Battn in the line. Relieved by 17th Welsh Regt in the front line & take over support battalion area vacated by them. Relief complete 11.30pm. B.H.Q. at R.31 a.0.0 A Coy R 26a 8.5 support coy to Left Battalion. B Coy R 31 6.6. C Coy R 32 a 9.9 D Coy R 26 d.4.3 support coy to Right Battn. Test S.O.S rockets (2) fired at 10pm.	
GOUZEAUCOURT	22nd		Battn in support. A.C.D. Corps find night working parties for RE tasks in new front line GONNELIEU SECTOR. Capt Gilbey (attached) to Division 2/Lt L.J. Turnbull off leave.	
"	23rd		Battn in support. B. Coy find working party for R.E. task in front line trench, commencing at 6.30 a.m. Capt J.S. Jones returned from Rheinforcement Depot taken over command of B. Coy.	
"	24th		Battn in support. Casualties. 4 O.R. sick	
"	25th		Battn in support D Coy find working party for RE task in front line trench commencing at 6.30 a.m. 2nd Lieut. Rogers J.P, Whib J.J and Lewis S R report for duty. Casualties 1 O.R. sick.	
"	26th		Battn in support. Casualties 1 OR sick. wounded	
"	27th		Battn in support. Capt W.D. Ballgak goes on leave to England. Captain S.E. McClatchey took over duty as P.M.O during his absence. Casualties 3 OR sick.	A.I.J.

Vol 15

War Diary
18th (S) Bn (The Welch Regt.

August 1917

Army Form C. 2118

WAR DIARY
or
INTELLIGENCE SUMMARY
(Erase heading not required.)

Place	Date	Hour	Summary of Events and Information	Remarks and references to Appendices
GOUZEAUCOURT	28th		Batt⁴ in Support.	
	29th		Batt⁴ in Support. Relieved 15th K.R.R. Right Sub Sector/ 18HQ R.26 d. 6.7. GONNELIEU 2 Companies in front line: 2 Companies in Support. (A & C Coy) Casualties: 1 O.R. Sick.
GONNELIEU	30th		Batt⁴ in the Line. The Rev. Capt. Tomkins attached. Casualties: 1 O.R. Sick.	
"	31st		Batt⁴ in the Line.	

Menne
Lt. Col.
Comdg 15th Bn H.L.I. & Welsh Rgt.

Army Form C. 2118.

WAR DIARY
or
INTELLIGENCE SUMMARY.

(Erase heading not required.)

Instructions regarding War Diaries and Intelligence Summaries are contained in F.S. Regs., Part II. and the Staff Manual respectively. Title pages will be prepared in manuscript.

Place	Date	Hour	Summary of Events and Information	Remarks and references to Appendices
Gonnelieu	1/8/17		Battn in the Line.	
"	2/8/17		Battn in the Line. A raiding party consisting of 3 officers and 81 O.R's went to the gap in the Enemy wire at about R.28.a.0.5. (57c) they were met by a hostile party and, after a bombing encounter, returned to our line. 12 prisoners who were in charge was wounded also 13 O.Rs	
GRANTHAM	3/8/17		Battn relieved by the 12th Suffolk Regt. Relief completed by 1 p.m. Battn went into Reserve at GRANTHAM Suffolk TERRACE W6 a 6.4 (57c). During the right of the 3rd/4th Battn relieved the 17th Welsh Regt in the Right sub sector VILLERS Plouich. It 'A' down reported back from Granges '£B' pop in front line, 'B&D' pop in Support. Battn.	
VILLERS PLOUICH.	4/8/17		Battn in the Line. 'A' & 'C' coys in the Line. D.Q.R.H. C8.00. (57c)	
	5/6/17		Battn in the Line	
	6/8/17		Battn in the Line. Relieved by the 17th Welsh Regt at 11 p.m. Battn went into Reserve at GRANTHAM Suffolk TERRACE.	

Army Form C. 2118.

WAR DIARY
or
INTELLIGENCE SUMMARY.
(Erase heading not required.)

Instructions regarding War Diaries and Intelligence Summaries are contained in F. S. Regs., Part II. and the Staff Manual respectively. Title pages will be prepared in manuscript.

Place	Date	Hour	Summary of Events and Information	Remarks and references to Appendices
GRANTHAM. Suffolk Terrace	8/8/17		Buffs in Reserve. Lt Col W Kennedy goes on leave.	
"	9/8/17		Batt. in Reserve.	
"	10/8/17		Batt. in Reserve	
"	11/8/17		Batt. in Reserve.	
"	12/8/17		Batt. in Reserve	
"	13/8/17		Batt. in Reserve	
"	14/8/17		Batt. in Reserve.	
"	15/8/17		Batts Relieved 17. Welsh in the Brigade Left subsector. The Relief was completed by 10.55 pm.	
VILLERS PLOUICH. Pinesight.	16/8/17		Batts in the Line.	
	17/8/17		Batts in the Line. 2nd Lieut Bowen and one OR (Private Bryan) went out on a daylight patrol to the CEMETERY. (La Vacquerie)	
	18/8/17		Batt. in the Line.	
	19/8/17		Batts in the Line	
	20/8/17		Batts in the Line. Lt Col W Kennedy returns from leave.	
	21/8/17		Batts in The Line	
	22/8/17		Batts in the Line. Patrol to encounter North Patrol 2nd Lt Whatley wounded	

WAR DIARY
or
INTELLIGENCE SUMMARY.
(Erase heading not required.)

Army Form C. 2118.

Place	Date	Hour	Summary of Events and Information	Remarks and references to Appendices
VILLERS PLOUICH	23/8/17		Batt. in the line. Relieved by the 17th Welsh Regt on the night of the 23/24th. Regt relief complete 10.30. Batt. went into reserve at Suffock Reserve	
"Revelon" Suffolk Reserve	24th 8/17		Batt. in reserve	
	25/8/17		Batt. in reserve	
	26/8/17		Batt. in reserve. No Reports	
	27/8/17		Batt. in reserve	
	28/8/17		Batt. in reserve	
	29/8/17		Batt. in reserve. B.H.Q. moved to the Gouzeaucourt Trescault Road c at Q.30.d.8.8.	
GOUZEAUCOURT TRESCOURT RD	30/8/17		Battalion in Reserve.	
	31/8/17		Battalion in Reserve. The Battalion relieved the 17th Bn. the Welsh Regt. in the Left Sub Sector. VILLERS-PLOUICH on night of 31/1/Aug. Relief complete at 9.55 p.m.	

31-8-17

Mayo
Lt. Col.
Comdg. 19 Welch Regt

Vol 16

War Diary

18th (S) Bn. 17th Welch Regiment

September 1917

16.E.
13 sheets

16.E.

Army Form C. 2118.

WAR DIARY
or
INTELLIGENCE SUMMARY.
(Erase heading not required.)

1st (5th) Bn. Welsh Regt.

Instructions regarding War Diaries and Intelligence Summaries are contained in F. S. Regs., Part II. and the Staff Manual respectively. Title pages will be prepared in manuscript.

Place	Date	Hour	Summary of Events and Information	Remarks and references to Appendices
VILLERS-PLOUICH	1/9/17		Regt. Specialist GOUZEAUCOURT 5-9-17 1/2-1-0 (Lt-Col. Rector) Battalion in the Line: Batt. Headquarters R.20.a.20.90. B. Company - Right Front (H.Q. R.20.a.70.80) D. Company - Right Support do C. Company - Left Front (H.Q. R.17.d.10.90) A. do - Left Support (H.Q. R.14.a.80.85) Hostile artillery retaliation. Daylight patrol carried out by 2 officers on CORNER REDOUBT to reconnoitre new line from RISE 20. to officer. Lieut. W.B. RODERICK reported back from III CORPS REST STATION. Captain C.E. SANKEY do do do to 47th Div. 17th B.F. School, 8 O.R.'s from duty as Postmen/Orderlies. 1 O.R. to duty from 40 Div. Signal School. 1 O.R. to Hospital (Dental Treatment)	
	2/9/17		Battalion in Line. Enemy Quiet- several French Mortars activity. Considerably amount of work on trenches. Wire improved in front of ADVANCED LINE (MELSH TRENCH) to right of LAVAQUERIE CEMETERY ROAD. Work parties from 1/4 Welsh (Battalion in Reserve) worked on trenches improvement during the night	
	3/9/17		Patrol examined enemy wire at about R.15.c.50.60 - crossed to fairly strong W. of SHEPHERDS-PRISE. Found wires in trenches. 1 N.C.O. attached to Mining Company with 231 st Field Company, R.E. 3 O.R's to Hospital Sick. 2nd Lieut E.S. LEES and 8 O.R.'s returning from not Regimental School at DAOURS.	

Army Form C. 2118.

WAR DIARY
or
INTELLIGENCE SUMMARY.
(Erase heading not required.)

Place	Date	Hour	Summary of Events and Information	Remarks and references to Appendices
VILLERS-PLOUICH	1/9/17		Battalion in the Line: Inter Company Relief: "D" Company - Right front	
			"B" do - Right support	
			"A" do - Left front	
			"C" do - Left support	
			Patrol work considerably hampered by bright moonlight. Enemy fairly Quiet. Trench mortar active from time to time.	
			Reinforcements of 59 o.r. from R.S. I.B.D. received much.	
			Captain B.B. McSTLAKE RAMC attached 135th Field Ambulance relieved Captain R.B. McCLATCHY RAMC as Regimental M.O.	
			2nd Lieut T.G. WHITE } Returned from Bayonet Bombing and	
			2nd Lieut S.F. PERROTT } LMG Schol, NURLU	
			19 o.r. returned do	
			2nd Lieut T.T. BOWEN and # Lieut I.I. LAWRENCE	
			20 o.r. proceeded to Brigade School, NURLU.	
			Work to be proceeded with - Widening Russian Bevways. Improvements to wire - thickening Improvements to wire - thickening mainly to be kept on night to	
			Improvements to mine - thickening	
			in metal and moral warn takes during the night	
5/9/17			Battalion in the line. Condition normal as regards Enemy Action. Toy Up relief and arrangements to reconnoitre encounter with troops at approx R15 c 6 80. No active enemy artillery.	

A.8834 Wt.W4973/M687 750,000 8/16 D. D. & L. Ltd. Forms/C.2118/13.

WAR DIARY or INTELLIGENCE SUMMARY

Army Form C. 2118.

Place	Date	Hour	Summary of Events and Information	Remarks and references to Appendices
VILLERS-PLOUICH	5/9/17		(Continued) Major C.C. DOWDING proceeded on 11 days leave to the United Kingdom. 1 o.r. w/officer been sent to BRIGADE SCHOOL, NURLU. Causes: do do do do do Inspector. 2 Lieut G.V. JONES proceeded to do do do do do in Bombing. 1 o.r. Returned from Transport Course at ABBEVILLE.	
	6/9/17		H.Q.R. to Morfikel – Lick's. Improvement to trenches. Lyn H Trench Barrs, widening and deepening trenches. Wire taken down last night by 13" Welsh Regt. working in French environment on Advanced Line string along the front. detached belt of wire. Fighting patrol out and reported enemy wire in R15central and CORNER REDOUBT (R15c8). There is an empty trench high belt along west of enemy front East of the Allemes. Lieut P.A. LEWIS proceeded on leave (11 days) to the U.K. via Le Havre. 2 n.o. 2 R.o. 3 o.r. to repaired Lick 1 o.r. returned from Nurlu Sig. attacked 231 NZ SCh/5 RE. 1 o.r. from Morfikel.	
	7/9/17		Patrol sent out to confirm above report re wire at Corner Redoubt. Work improved with; 1 o.r. proceed on 11 days leave to U.K. L/C G.E. LEWIS returned to unit from AOXW 1274 B.E. school, NURLU. Also 2 n.s.R.	

WAR DIARY
or
INTELLIGENCE SUMMARY.

Army Form C. 2118.

Place	Date	Hour	Summary of Events and Information	Remarks and references to Appendices
VILLERS-PLOUICH	9/9/17		The Battalion was relieved by the 14th W. Lit. Regt. Relief completed 10 p.m. Battalion returned to RESERVE BILLETS. B.H.Q. in Beaucamp Road Q.30.d.75.90. "A" Company in Sunken Rd. Q.30.c.40.95. "B" do QUENTIN MILL. R.31.d.20.30. "C" do do do "D" do Reserve Rd. Q.30.d.75.95. 2 ORs on leave to United Kingdom 3 ORs to Hospital (Sick) 1 OR returned from Hospital	
GOUZEAUCOURT.	9/9/17		Battalion in Brigade Reserve. Commanec Bakers at 40th Division at Bath. GOUZEAUCOURT: Cleaning Equipment. Marie Cattrar attended R.E. for class on BILLET Improvement. 1 OR on leave to Signal Zinglow. 12.60 – 6 ORs attached for Brigade Tunnelling Sections in rear. Half dug-out at Reserve Billets 2 ORs to Hospital (Sick) 2 ORs returned from Hospital	
	10/9/17		Battalion in Reserve. Companies paraded during afternoon for musketry and wiring Practice. Work Parties proceeded during night to work on Front Line Trenches. Left Sub-Sector – Improvement.	

WAR DIARY
or
INTELLIGENCE SUMMARY.

Army Form C. 2118.

Place	Date	Hour	Summary of Events and Information	Remarks and references to Appendices
GOUZEAUCOURT	10/9/17	(continued)	1 Company working by day – "cleaning up" – in Advanced Front Line Trench. 1 O.R. on leave to U.K. 9 O.R. returned from leave to U.K. (2 O.Rs. to Hospital (Sick))	
	11/9/17		Musketry Practice – Wiring – Cleaning up of Trenches of O.R. in Rapid wire. Work parties proceeded to Front Line Trench – cleaning up, draining, widening trenches, bombing. Plevie Patrol sent out to thoroughly reconnoitre wire at ORANGE REDOUBT and to push on if possible & through to Enemy Garrison in connection with proposed raid. 1 O.R. home on U.K. leave. 1 O.R. returned from leave to U.K. 1 O.R. to Hospital (wounded) 1 O.R. admitted to Hospital.	#4
	12/9/17		Musketry & Wiring Practice. Work parties in Front Line Trenches. 3 Companies by night – one Company by day. Lieut. Col. [?] and party in training at Hargone Central Works. Road Posts went and party in training to Ytres.	

Army Form C. 2118.

WAR DIARY
or
INTELLIGENCE SUMMARY.
(Erase heading not required.)

Place	Date	Hour	Summary of Events and Information	Remarks and references to Appendices
GOUZEAUCOURT	12/9/17	(Continued)	1 OR proceeded on leave to UK. 3 ORs returned from leave. 1 OR returned from Veterinary Course, ABBEVILLE. 3 ORs returned from Hospital. 1 OR to Hospital (Sick).	
	13/9/17	In Reserve.	Training during the afternoon. War Trophies to Front Line Barracks. Lieut. F. PASCOE proceeded to DOUZEENS re Divisional representative. R.F.C. re transfer. 1 OR leave to UK. 2 OR to Hospital (Sick).	
	14/9/17	In Reserve.	Raining during afternoon. Boundaries marked in front line trenches by night - 1 Company by day. 3 ken 26/6 (actual war). 1 OR on leave to UK. 1 OR returned from leave to UK. 1 OR proceeded for attachment to 110 T.M. Battery for course of instruction. 3 ORs returned from Hospital. 7 ORs to Hospital (6 sick and 1 S.I.W.)	
	15/9/17	In Reserve.	Spent in trucking and ferrying. 36 Companies parties to Front Line Benches during this night - One Company carrying all day on improvements to trenches.	

A5834 Wt. W4973/M687 750,000 8/16 D. D. & L. Ltd. Forms/C.2118/13.

WAR DIARY or INTELLIGENCE SUMMARY

Army Form C. 2118.

Place	Date	Hour	Summary of Events and Information	Remarks and references to Appendices
GOUZEAUCOURT	13/9/17	(Continued)	1 NCO Leave to UK. 2nd Lieutenant from III Corps Bombing School. 2nd August 17. Captain N.J. BATHGATE, RAMC, Regimental Unit as Regimental MO and relieves Captain B.B. WESTLAKE, RAMC, who returned to 135th 2 A.M. Firms. 1 OR to Hospital (Flu). North parties out supplies on right front to b'let.	
	14/9/17		Baths: Bath Commenced at GOUZEAUCOURT BATHS. Relieved 11th Worcs Regt in the Right Sub Section, VILLERS PLOUICH. Complete by 9-30 pm. Battalion HQ: R20 a 20.90. "B" Company — Right Front "D" do Left do "C" Company Right Support "A" do Left do Av. do – do do PONT RENY	
VILLERS-PLOUICH	15/9/17		Battalion in the Line: Weather Condition Fair. Enemy Quiet. Normal Routine not Misbehaviour proceeded with. Patrol sent out to Locate Hostile M.G. with P.I.C.O. to position free from Enemy. Patrol fired upon from P19 c 55 to w 8. R15 a 15 55 by Night M.G. 12 ORs returned from hospital (Leave) 2 ORs Re turned from Hospital 4 ORs to Hospital (Sick) 2nd Lieut F PASCOE returned from DOULLENS.	

Army Form C. 2118.

WAR DIARY
or
INTELLIGENCE SUMMARY.
(Erase heading not required.)

Instructions regarding War Diaries and Intelligence Summaries are contained in F. S. Regs., Part II. and the Staff Manual respectively. Title pages will be prepared in manuscript.

Place	Date	Hour	Summary of Events and Information	Remarks and references to Appendices
VILLE RS- PLOUICH	18/9/17		Battalion in the line. Work continued on front line and wire. 2nd Lieut. R.F.W. PEEL returned from Lewis Gun P. & P.B.S. School. OR returned from 40th Div. P & B. School. 2nd Lieut. O.B. MARKHAM proceeded to 40th Div. Signalling School. 11 OR	
			2 OR wounded (accidentally) to Hospital 4 OR " OR (BAHD) 20 2 ORs (RUM) 20 3 ORs returned from Hospital	
In the line	19/9/17		Became dull & quite wet from 14:00 onwards but the (NORTH-WESTERLY) succeeded with... wind so Passion... movement to June Lake - Several Bombards P6 & Patrols sent to reconnoitre enemy... to man's land... Captain J. R. WILLIAMS returned from Company Commanders Course at JARNY. 1 OR OTHER party to Lant, Auch... CHATEAU 4 OR returned to Hospital (Sick)	
In the line	20/9/17		Work on Barbed... went... wiring... digging of shelters... men occupied kays. Patrol sent out to reconnoitre wire at R150.a.6 to R150.a.5 Along general lines given. Party Lieut... on Trench Mortar (double Explosion) and... first to Rifle Grenades (instant detonator) and ammunition needed were fired towards Enemy Trenches at Carnoy Branch. 2nd Lieut. T. J. BOWEN returned from Bombing School renew 20:00	

WAR DIARY
or
INTELLIGENCE SUMMARY

Army Form C. 2118.

Place	Date	Hour	Summary of Events and Information	Remarks and references to Appendices
VILLERS-PLOUICH	20/9/17	(continued)	Major A.C. DOWDING returned from leave to the Unit) King form Lieut P.A. LEWIS do do 1 O.R. do do Lieut I.T. LAWRENCE } proceeded to L.M.G. Course at Brigade School NURLU 5 O.R's do do do 10 O.R's. to Bombing Course do do 4 O.R's to Signalling do. do do 1 O.R. to Hospital (sick) (S.I.W)	
	21/9/17	In the Line	Work on wire, Fernahs and old Huns entrenchments continued. Work parties from 14 N.Z.Rifle Brigade, widening, deepening, widening + improving trenches. Battalion rewired (about 2 O.R's from Lewis M.R. 500 to the other (4 men 1 accidental) front Running, 3 at night)	
	22/9/17	In the Line	Work continued. Work parties from 14 N.Z.Rifle. The 14th H.L.I. M.P.L. 120 "B"/4 Brigade made a successful raid on Enemy Trenches (FARM. TR). supported by Artillery, M.G's and Trench Mortars. 2 x 4" Trench Mortars fired Preliminary bombardment of THERMITE shells. The attack afterwards was covered by a dense smoke barrage. Some Prisoners were taken. Our casualties very light. 2nd Lieut G.I. TURNBULL and 10 O.R. returned from Firing Course at AUXI-LE-CHATEAU.	

Army Form C. 2118.

WAR DIARY
or
INTELLIGENCE SUMMARY.
(Erase heading not required.)

Place	Date	Hour	Summary of Events and Information	Remarks and references to Appendices
VILLERS-PLOUICH	21/9/17	(Continued)	2 ORs returned from hospital. 5 ORs returned from hospital.	
	22/9/17	In the line	Work carried on in the trenches. Taking to improve wireless at R.31.d.2.07. Intercept found to be inoperative. Capt F PRYCE conducting. 3 ORs proceeded to No. 6 Inf Base HQ as Lewis Gunners. 1 OR to hospital (sick). 1 OR to Base. Advised PB. 1 OR wounded remaining at duty.	
	22/9/17	In the line	Bn Hdqrs moved to Reserve Bldgs at GOUZEAUCOURT. Released Lt Col B.W. Vann VC 1/8 Notts & Derby Regt. Capt E.M. EDWARDS proceed to Paris on leave (7 days). 3 ORs to hospital (sick). 1 OR on leave to U.K. Forwarded overseas by No. 2 I.B.D. 1 OR from No. 1 I.B.D.	
GOUZEAUCOURT	23/9/17	Battalion in Reserve	Battery at GOUZEAUCOURT B.47.4.5. Claiming up Requirements. Dumps turned in for reserve bivouacs in blocks. 3 ORs returned (sick) from 3rd ARMY Laundry, Boisleux. 3 ORs to hospital (sick).	
	24/9/17	In Reserve.	The Battalion was on work parties on Gouzeaucourt Corcaus - Hermies (interior) road trams - night - carrying tracks & ammunition - sentries. Lt Col T PHILLIPS and 100 Reinforcements from III Corps Rest Station, CERISY BAILLY. 1 OR leave to U.K. 3 ORs to hospital (1 wounded 1 S.I.W. and 1 sick). 3 ORs to hospital & admitted from HQ to hospital. 133 ORs Reinforcement from No. 6 I.B.D. ROUEN. Arrived at allotted to III Corps Training Camps. HAUT ALLAINES.	

WAR DIARY or INTELLIGENCE SUMMARY

Army Form C. 2118.

Place	Date	Hour	Summary of Events and Information	Remarks and references to Appendices
GOUZEAUCOURT	24/9/17		Musketry firing – Bivouac – wiring – Inspection during afternoon. 1 Bombing working party on front line trenches 83 hours by day do do by night. 3 do do do do do 1 OR to hospital (wounded) 2 ORs returned from hospital.	
	25/9/17	In Reserve	Raining continued through the morning. Work parties as usual. 4 ORs to Hospital (Sick). 2 NCOs Reinforcements & Report for duty from M Infantry DEPOT Details Training Camp, HAUT ALLAINES	
	26/9/17	In Reserve	Fine. Work parties as usual. Capt. E.W. EDWARDS returned from PARIS leave. 2/Lieut E.S. LEECE & others returned from leave at PT.P. 2/Lieut. J.H. CURTIS proceeded on 3rd Army L.M.G. School LESTOUVE. Captain (H.E.) SANKEY and 2 ORs to 2nd Army Infantry School AUXI-LE-CHATEAU 1 OR to Scouting & Observing Company School Ain. –– re CHATEAU 2 Lieut. M.B. RODERICK) Proceeded to III Corps Training Camp 3 NCOs) the nation Anglais HAUT ALLAINES to matine Drafts. 2nd Lieut M.B. DAVIES – attached 119 T.M. Battery – returned from hospital. 3 ORs returned from hospital. 1 OR to hospital (sick)	
	27/9/17			

Army Form C. 2118.

WAR DIARY
or
INTELLIGENCE SUMMARY.
(Erase heading not required.)

Place	Date	Hour	Summary of Events and Information	Remarks and references to Appendices
GOUZEAUCOURT	30/9/17		Training and work parties as usual. Lieut F J BOREN and 201 proceeded to (?) Bn/o HQ for attachment to Corps Heavy Artillery for 6 weeks. 2 ORs returned from Hospital. 2 ORs to Hospital (Sick). 25 ORs Reinforcement to reported for duty from No 6 IBD.	Maurice Holt Capt 15 Welsh

WAR DIARY

18th (S) Bn. The Welsh Regt

October 1917

WAR DIARY
or
INTELLIGENCE SUMMARY.

(Erase heading not required.)

Army Form C. 2118.

Place	Date	Hour	Summary of Events and Information	Remarks and references to Appendices
GOUZEAUCOURT.	1/10/17	In Reserve.	Three Companies on work in the Front line trenches during the night - trench improvement and drains. — One company by day. Musketry training and working parties. Two O.Rs to hospital Sick. — One O.R returned from III Corps School. Four O.Rs from Hospital.	
	2/10/17	In Reserve.	The Battalion Bathed at GOUZEAUCOURT BATHS. Relieved 17th Welch Regt. in the Left Sub. Sector VILLERS PLOUICH. Relief completed by 8.40 p.m. Battalion H.Q. R.29.a.20.90. "B" Company — Right Front. " A " — Left " " C " — Right Support " D " — Left Support Eight men to Hospital Sick. Three men returned from Hospital.	
	3/10/17	In the Line.	Battn continued working on the Shelters in the Front line and generally repairing trenches and parapets. One O.R. killed in water by Shell Fire. Enemy attempted to raid Brigade on our Right. Three O.Rs to hospital. 2nd Lieut. FRASER & an O.R. went to 3rd Army Musketry School PONT REMY.	

WAR DIARY
or
INTELLIGENCE SUMMARY.

Army Form C. 2118.

Place	Date	Hour	Summary of Events and Information	Remarks and references to Appendices
In the Line.	4/10/17		Night T.M. fire during the day. Work continued with "A" Coy company relief. Three O.R. classified as P.B. sent to the 6/2 R.D. Two to Hospital sick. Two O.R. leave to U.K. (4th-15th)	
In the Line.	5/10/17		A party consisting of two officers and 60 O.R.s with R.E. made a raid on the enemy trenches in R152. The Party were covered by a S.T. & Third Patrol under 2nd Lieut Robinson. The Raiding Party was in charge of Captain J.F. Jnr. They entered the enemy trenches killing four 5 or 6 garrison of the trench two dugouts. The party returned bringing a Prussian Swine. Only five of our Raiding Party were wounded in action. Captain William J. Parker O.B.E. commanded the O.R. killed in action. Three O.R.s returned home to U.K. Col. Kennaway Esq. Lieut Frankhaus + 12 O.R.s returned from the Brigade Specialty courses. Lance Cpl J. Fila went to England to Cadet School.	

Place	Date	Hour	Summary of Events and Information	Remarks and references to Appendices
In the Line.	6/10/17		Lewis Gunnery 17M nongquet. Three Officers of the R.B. Course to the band and started to take over the Batt's front. G.S.O.I. of the 59th Div'n greeted on from their trenches. Two men returned from hospital. Two men (key in P.O) Cong.St. Hot Div. Run reported for duty. Eight men to Hospital sick. One OR on leave UKR (6th & 7th)	
In the Line.	7/10/17		Batt's relieved by the 11th R.B. relief complete by 10-40 am. the Batt's moving to Camp at Rafah. Transport trains remaining at this. Six men from the M.B.E. Brigade Tunnelling Company. Four employees from the Brigade School NER I.V. also two Instructors. Lieut. Lawrence proceeded 2d O.R.s returned from Brigade School NER I.V. Four O.R.s from the 119th French Mor. Bty. 2nd Lieut Pascoe a bomb to each on leave. One OR wounded to Hospital. Two O.R.s to Hospital sick. One OR returned from Hospital.	

Army Form C. 2118.

WAR DIARY
or
INTELLIGENCE SUMMARY.
(Erase heading not required.)

Place	Date	Hour	Summary of Events and Information	Remarks and references to Appendices
RAILTON	8/10/17		Battn at RAILTON. The Battn entrained by Decauville at 2 p.m. for PERONNE. Detrained at St Denis and marched to camp at PERONNE arriving by 3.30 p.m. Transport moved by Road March from FINS to new billets. One man in camp WUK (8/3/17). One man returned from Hospital Sick. Two O.R's returned from Tropical ac. One man to hospital sick. Five O.R's reported from III Corps Training Camp HAUT ALLAINES	
PERONNE	9/10/17		2 Battn (Cadres) at PERONNE 3rd Corps 62* in Field Batt Officer Comdg and presented ribbons to 2/Lieut G.V. Jones y N°40690 Private Jennings W.E. (M.C. & M.M. respectively) 2nd Lieut R.A. Lewis & one O.R. reported to Staff Captain 114th Infantry Brigade at 4 a.m. as billeting party. 2nd Lieut F. Pascoe reported to Royal Flying Corps attached. With strength of the Battn. Two O.R's reported for duty from 6 g. LBD. Five men to Hospital sick. One returned from Road Control. Two from Hospital. Sgn. O.R. ½ …. …. Brigade	

WAR DIARY
or
INTELLIGENCE SUMMARY.
(Erase heading not required.)

Army Form C. 2118.

Place	Date	Hour	Summary of Events and Information	Remarks and references to Appendices
PERONNE	19/10/17		Battalion moved by train to GOUY-EN-ARTOIS. Training as "A" Coy and arrived at destination at 2-30. Transport to the first half arriving at destination the morning before moving. Left PERONNE at 10AM.Train arrived from BEAUMONT-HAM- LOGES & GOUY-EN-ARTOIS was our new HQ. March route to Billets. The remainder of H.Q. transport left PERONNE at 6AM and moved by Road to BAPAUME where they had Billets for the night.108/11R. (in charge of Major C.E. Bosley M.C.) B.H.Q. arrived in from at Cross Roads near GOUY-EN- ARTOIS (Sheet 57c. 12-18-a 8-4) All four Companies and Trans. have in the village of GOUY-EN-ARTOIS. Lieut. W.White went to No.6. I.B.D - 2nd Lieut. J.T.Phillips to England to 6 months tour of duty. One OR on leave to U.K. One OR to hospital.	
GOUY-EN-ARTOIS.	20/10/17		The day was spent in cleaning up and inspecting kits. The men were paid and two Companies and HO Staff bathed. The remainder of the Transport arrived at 2pm from BAPAUME in charge of Major C.E. Bagley M.C. Two OR went to Hospital. One OR on leave to U.K. (No 262201) from - returned from -	

WAR DIARY
or
INTELLIGENCE SUMMARY

Army Form C. 2118.

Place	Date	Hour	Summary of Events and Information	Remarks and references to Appendices
GOUY-EN-ARTOIS	12/10/17		Elementary training with Arms and Batt: Parade. Coy Commanders took over. Work was done by Coys in Company training grounds and Sports field. Certain bays improvement continued with. Draft 65 other OR's from NoG IBD. Two returned from Hospital. One OR on leave 2 UK (12th- 23rd) One OR to Hospital.	
	13/10/17		Rout: Parade in the morning. Work on kits continued. 2 in Company football matches in the afternoon. One OR to Hospital	
	14/10/17		Church Parade on Battn: Parade ground. R.C. at Village Church. No other parade. Two N.C.O went to Brigade School Sandhurst as Instructors in Bombing + Lewis M. Gun. Ten OR's employed at Brigade School BRUNEHNET. 15 OR's also for Instruction.	
	15/10/17		Batt: out on training. Sympathy in the Afternoon. The father Divisional were presented on Batt: Parade. MILITARY MEDALS to No 24679 Sergeant B DELANEY. Sergt: Delaney Served Parliamen and was a few Months in arrest on 5th Oct: 1917. Three of his comrades who took in disabling the _____	

A5834 Wt. W4973/M687 759,000 8/16 D. D. & L. Ltd. Forms/C.2118/13.

WAR DIARY
or
INTELLIGENCE SUMMARY.
(Erase heading not required.)

Army Form C. 2118.

Place	Date	Hour	Summary of Events and Information	Remarks and references to Appendices
GOUY-EN-ATOIS	16/10/17		The raiding party employed in training with the instructor. Also No. 449721 Private E.J. CORNISH arrived on the Evening train on 5th October 1917. After his departure in charge of sub-men in early morning raid on CORNISH to lot seen. Evidently Evidently raid we never heard the Enemy firing and the 2nd party wish to watch the Enemy Group played until quite outside was 5ft 6 from the Divisional Depot played with Divisional Brig 10th Batts At 6 p.m. General quiet in the Divisional Front 10th Batts at 6 P.m. One O.R. Returned from Hospital.	
"	17/10/17		Batt: Training. Arm drill. P.T. Company drill. All four Companies paraded. 119th Brigade Armorer inspected L.M.G. and Rifles of the Batt: reported them all in good condition. Four Officers left for DOULLENS on leave for the day returning at 7 pm. Two O.R's for Bombing course and two O.R. for Stokes Gun Course to HUMBERCAMP. One Lost. to train Gun Course at LA CAUCHIE. One O.R on Leave U.K (16th - 26th). One O.R. to Hospital. Two O.R's returned from Hospital. Training continued with the Batt: football team was defeated by K 136 Field Ambulance in the Divisional football contest. Batt: paid by Companies on the Batt Rifle Range. Two O.R's to Hospital sick. Lieut Lorimer sent to Hospital sick.	

Army Form C. 2118.

WAR DIARY
or
INTELLIGENCE SUMMARY.
(Erase heading not required.)

Place	Date	Hour	Summary of Events and Information	Remarks and references to Appendices
Gouy.GN. ATRIUS	18/10/17		Training continued. Rifle Range completed and second one started. Musketry Lectures to Officers and N.C.O's in the evening. One OR to hospital sick. Head braches and "A" Company baths. Baths carried on the Coy day.	
Gouy.GN. ATRIUS	19/10/17		Route march by the Battalion. Officers and N.C.O's to a reconnaissance with the Comdg Officer. "B" & "C" Company bathed in the afternoon. 2nd Lieut. L.G. Lewis awarded the MILITARY CROSS "On the 5th October 1917 this Officer guided his raiding party to the point of Assembly, and to the gap in the enemy's wire. He was the first to enter the enemy's trenches and although stunned by a trench explosion on returning he led his party forward with coolness and determination and continued clearing the trenches until recalled." Coy Officers go on one day tour to BOUZEAUX-leaving at 8 am and returning at 4.5 pm. Engineers commence work on the wood of "D" Company billet. O.C. O.R's hospital cadre. The R.P.S.M of course Wik K.M.18. Three OR's evacuated from Leave. 2 N.C.O's returned from Musketry.	
	20/10/17		Training in the Church placed on Battalions command of the G.O.C. 119th Infantry Brigade inspected the Battalion and remarked "After 45 and Lieut L.G. Lewis." Company Comdr inspected Commdt Officer inspected the ground over which the brigade attack is to take place in the afternoon. Captain T. McMahon on Leave 5 UK (10-30)	

WAR DIARY
or
INTELLIGENCE SUMMARY.

(Erase heading not required.)

Army Form C. 2118.

Place	Date	Hour	Summary of Events and Information	Remarks and references to Appendices
	20/10/17	(cont.)	Four O.R's to Hospital Sick. Three returned non ill to hospital. A draft of 12 O.R's from No 6 I.B.D. Two O.R's to Army Rest camp.	
GODEWAERSVELDE.	21/10/17		Church Parade in the Buteaux's parade ground at 9 (915) P.18. C. with Brigade arrangements. R.E. attended service in village church. Football matches (inter Company) were played during the afternoon, watched by Comdg Officer & Officers and O.Rs of Coy. & O. & the Brigadry. One O.R. returned from 3rd Army Sanitary Course. Three O.R's " " " Hospital	
"	22/10/17		Batt. training in fighting Water formations. The scheme of carrying out party of attack. Secondly inter platoon arrangements, Thirdly by Companies. Special instructions given in the afternoon. One O.R returned from leave. One O.R " " " Hospital	
"	23/10/17		Field day under Brigade Arrangement. The Brigade in attack. The Batt. marched off at 8.30 AM and took up its position in Q.U.C. at Q.15 AM. Zero hour 10 AM. The Batt. was detailed	

WAR DIARY or INTELLIGENCE SUMMARY

Army Form C. 2118.

Place	Date	Hour	Summary of Events and Information	Remarks and references to Appendices
			As follows the 17th Bttn. and K attacked a first objective. The ground between the Transvay (?) and K and our objective was marked on 4 with strong points. The Bttn's objective was reached at 12.15 p.m. The Bttn. assembled back up to Bttn. at 12.30 p.m. Our N.C.O. went to the North Dorsets (Headquarters at SAILLY) on O.R. on leave B.4.R. (23rd & 24th Nov.) Two O.R.'s reported to the Brigade School. Our O.R. returned from hospital.	
HOUPLIN ANCOISNE	24/11/17		The Brigade was inspected by the G.O.C. 40 Division at Q.H. & Coll. The inspection and march past took place at 3 p.m. The Officers and N.C.O. died and rested Schemes will Coy. Officer in the morning Bttn's cleaning and preparing for inspection. One O.R. to Hospital. One O.R. returned from Hospital. Three O.R. returned from No. 6 Divisional Reinforcement Depot SAILLY. Draft of 25 O.R. from No. 6 I.B.D. One O.R. to No. 6 I.B.D. Classified P.B. One O.R. to Hospital from leave.	

WAR DIARY
or
INTELLIGENCE SUMMARY.

Place	Date	Hour	Summary of Events and Information	Remarks and references to Appendices
GOUY EN ARTOIS.	25/10/17		The Brigade practised the Attack on Bois the open ground NORTH OF LINENCOURT. The Batt. marched out at 2 a.m. and remained in Brigade reserve on the Zero +1.30. They then passed through the objectives of the 17th week. and on Zero + 3.30 were on to the last objective a distance roughly of 2000 + 1100 yds. Batt. returned to billets at 2.15. Pay Parades during the afternoon. Three OR returned from hospital. One OR off to 2/5 Rft. on leave to U.K. One OR from hospital.	
	26/10/17		Battalion training in Rifle Grenade and Lewis Gun work – Musketry – All four Companies bathed. The sports were postponed owing to the weather. The Divisional Band played in the Boring Shed at 8.30 p.m. Batt. Boxing Competition commenced training also for Divisional inter relievers. Three OR returned from Hospital. One OR att. 2/1 R.F. on leave to U.K.	
	27/10/17		Attack practised by Companies. Training in L.M.G. + Rifleman. Football match in the afternoon. Final of the Batt. Boxing Competition in the evening. Pte WILD represented the Batt. against Cpl MILLS R. Fus 12 S. W. B. in a air senior contest and won. Pte Rennie (light weight) against the 22 Scots won his contest against a rival of the 9/R Rennet.	

A 5834 Wt. W4973/M68 D. 050,000 8/16 D.D. & L. Ltd. Forms/C.2118/13. (10146646)

Army Form C. 2118.

WAR DIARY
or
INTELLIGENCE SUMMARY.
(Erase heading not required.)

Place	Date	Hour	Summary of Events and Information	Remarks and references to Appendices
GOUY EN ARTOIS	27/10/17 (cont)		Ten OR's to Hospital sick. Six OR's returned from Hospital. Twenty OR's returned from the Brigade School (including 2 Lt Hulands) MONCHIET. 2nd Lieut Q.V. Jones returned from Brigade School. 2nd Lieut R.S. Junkison returned from Hospital.	
	28/10/17		Church Parade in the morning. C of E on Batt parade ground. R.C. in village Church. Rugby football match against 1st Suff. Batt. Advanced party reported to 13 Bgde H.Q. at 12.41st pm. One OR's been B UR (29ii – 8vii/17). One OR returned from Division at receiving Batt faculty. Lieut P A Lewis aucun OR to hospital. Two OR returned from hospital.	
	29/10/17		The Batt: arrival by Rail. March from GOUY-EN-ARTOIS to LUCHEUX. The Batt: moved off at 8.15 A.M. and arrived at destination at about 12.30 p.m. Transport moved with the Batt: Seven to hospital sick. One other OR returned from sickness.	
LUCHEUX	30/10/17		The Batts did training in the morning. Section drill. Bayonet fighting. The afternoon was devoted to athletic games. Mr OP to Hospital (sick). Three returned from III Corps Army School Hospital. One OR returned from 4th Army Infantry Corps and arrived from 2 M.G. course at Touches	

Place	Date	Hour	Summary of Events and Information	Remarks and references to Appendices
Lucheux	31/10/17		Batt: training by Companies. Bayonet fighting, Physical drill and platoon drill. Rifle grenade firing and Bomb throwing in the afternoon. Brass Band attached to the WEST of the BOIS-a-POBERMONT. Batt: Concert party gave their first performance at 6 p.m. to 7 p.m. Two O.R.s returned from VII Corps T.M course at HUMBER Camp. two O.R.s returned from IVth Army rest Camp. Captain J.M. Mathias returned from leave. Lieut D. Salisbury reported for duty. One O.R. returned from Hospital.	

McKenny Lt Col
Comdg. 15th Batt R Welch Rfs

Army Form C. 2118.

119/40

119/13/2/

Vol 13

WAR DIARY
or
INTELLIGENCE SUMMARY.
(Erase heading not required.)

War Diary

18th (S) Bn. The Welsh Regiment

November 1917

WAR DIARY
or
INTELLIGENCE SUMMARY.

WAR DIARY.
INTELLIGENCE SUMMARY.
18th (Sv.) Batt. Welsh Regt.
NOVEMBER 1917.

WAR DIARY
or
INTELLIGENCE SUMMARY.
(Erase heading not required.)

Army Form C. 2118.

Place	Date	Hour	Summary of Events and Information	Remarks and references to Appendices
Lucknow	1/11/17		The Battn. marched out at 6.45 & training proceed West of Ban-de-RUBERMONT. Here they spent the day. Field Kitchens and Ammunition limbers accompanied the Battn. Two companies fired on the Range during the morning and the other two during the afternoon. Training in the use of the L.M.G. and Rifle Grenade was carried on with also special training in Buglers and scouts. The first round of the Divisional boxing competition was tonight. Wds. and Sgt. Hamm of this Battn. will fight in the 2nd round on Saturday. Two O.R. to hospital for dental treatment. One returned from hospital. One O.R. returned from leave.	
	2/11/17		The Battn. fired on the Lucknow range by companies. Two companies bathed in the morning and two in the afternoon. Divisional Band played a concert at 6 p.m. Three O.R. returned from hospital	
	3/11/17		Battn. practiced the attack on a woodland cleared common by rifle fire during the morning. Boxing and games during the afternoon. Bty parades. Lieut F.S. Leape and 7 O.R's on leave to U.K. (3rd-17th). One O.R. returned from hospital	

WAR DIARY or INTELLIGENCE SUMMARY

Army Form C. 2118.

Place	Date	Hour	Summary of Events and Information	Remarks and references to Appendices
LUCHEUX	4/11/17		Church of England service at 10 A.M. R.C. at Village church at 10.30 A.M. Games during the afternoon. Rugby football match against the S.W.B. at HUMBERCOURT. The L.W. Brown one kick to nothing. Eleven O.R's on leave to U.K. (4=19/8) One O.R returned from hospital. Captain G.E. Sankey and one O.R from Third Army School AUXI-LES-CHATEAUX.	
"	5/11/17		The Battn spent the day on the training ground. Company cookers went with the Battn. Two Companies used the range in the morning and two in the afternoon. Special training in the use of the No.23 Rifle Grenade and Lewis M. Gun was carried on with the Battn. One chief took 15 billets arriving at 4.15 P.M. Ten O.R's on leave to U.K. (5=19/8). Two O.R's to Hospital.	
"	6/11/17		The Battn fired during the morning on the LUCHEUX Range and and a scheme of "Outposts" was arranged for the afternoon which was attended by Divn. Twelve O.R's went on leave to U.K. (6=20/5) One O.R returned from leave. Three O.R's returned from hospital	R.S.

WAR DIARY
or
INTELLIGENCE SUMMARY.
(Erase heading not required.)

Army Form C. 2118.

Place	Date	Hour	Summary of Events and Information	Remarks and references to Appendices
Lucheux	7/10/17		Coy. Order & Kit Inspection. In the afternoon being assigned to games. 2nd Lieut. R.F.W. Rees and 9 O.R. went on leave to U.K. Draft of 6 N.C.O's arrived from N.6 I.B.D. One O.R. returned from hospital.	
	8/10/17		The Battn took part in a scheme with the 121st Brigade. The Battn was in Brigade Reserve. One man from Training Batts 2 Hospital Sick One O.R. returned from hospital. 9 O.R's went on leave to U.K. (8/12/25)	
	9/10/17		The Battn took part in scheme with 119th Brigade. "An Attack on the Bois de ROSSIGNOL". Battn was held in reserve - 11 O.R's went on leave to U.K. (9/1/25)	
	10/10/17		The Battn Bathed by Companies. Steadying Drill was carried out also Bayonet Fighting & P.J. during the morning. During the afternoon seventy Gunners of the Battn took part in a Brigade cross country run. The first Sgt Lt. Jno Battn coming in 7th Jno Battn country Butts was fourth. 2 OR's from VII Corps Course at HUMBERCAMP. 8 OR's went on leave to U.K.	

Army Form C. 2118.

WAR DIARY
or
INTELLIGENCE SUMMARY.
(Erase heading not required.)

Instructions regarding War Diaries and Intelligence Summaries are contained in F. S. Regs., Part II. and the Staff Manual respectively. Title pages will be prepared in manuscript.

Place	Date	Hour	Summary of Events and Information	Remarks and references to Appendices
LUCHEUX	11/11/17		Church Service (Rotestand) in the morning and evening. The Battn played football against the 17th Welsh and lost 10 pts to 5 nothing. Lieut Salisbury and 20 ORs to the IV Army School FIENCOURT. One OR returned from hospital. 6 ORs & 2nd Lieut E.A.R. Robinson went on leave to UK. (11" to 25")	
"	12/11/17		Brigade scheme. The Battn was detailed to chew the FOREST OF LUCHEUX. The Brigade assembled at on a line along the Road running North by South through Mre FRIE de la FONTAINE (57: 5W). The 12.S. W73. took the outpost line through which the advance was made against 19 R.W.F. were the Enemy. Seven ORs on leave to UK. (12" to 26".)	
	13/11/17		Battn spent the day on the training ground west of the BOIS DE ROBERMOUNT. Close and open order drill. Shooting and Grenade throwing were done. Scouts were practiced in The Wood. Captain Sankey and 2 ORs went to the Fourth Army Musketry School PONT-REMY. One OR from hospital. Seven ORs on leave to UK. (13" to 27".)	

Army Form C. 2118.

WAR DIARY
or
INTELLIGENCE SUMMARY.
(Erase heading not required.)

Instructions regarding War Diaries and Intelligence Summaries are contained in F.S. Regs., Part II. and the Staff Manual respectively. Title pages will be prepared in manuscript.

Place	Date	Hour	Summary of Events and Information	Remarks and references to Appendices
LUCHEUX	14/10/17		The Batt posted a rear guard action. The line of advance being Montreuil from LUCHEUX to Ht VSEE. Two platoons of "D" by motor lorries acted as the enemy. The first line of defence was taken up by "B" Coy North and South of the Road over the Railway in S30.6+d (57cSW) the 2nd line of defence being S28.G+d (57°SW) the afternoon was devoted to games. Concert in the Evening. Divisional band played during the afternoon. Two OR's went on leave to UK. Draft of 3 OR's from 116 & 1.B.D. One OR returned from hospital. The Batt took part in an advanced guard action. Troops responsible for the capture of the Bus de LUCHEUX. this woodwas taken in one hour and an "outpost" line was established on the Eastern side of the wood. The 17thWelch marched through us. Two OR to hospital and on returned. Two OR on leave to UK.	
LUCHEUX	16/10/17		The Batt left LUCHEUX for GOUY-EN-ATOIS at 6 AM and arrived at 10.30. Two OR's on leave to UK. Two OR's returned from Hospital	

Army Form C. 2118.

WAR DIARY
or
INTELLIGENCE SUMMARY.
(Erase heading not required.)

Instructions regarding War Diaries and Intelligence Summaries are contained in F. S. Regs., Part II. and the Staff Manual respectively. Title pages will be prepared in manuscript.

Place	Date	Hour	Summary of Events and Information	Remarks and references to Appendices
GOUY-en-ATH	17/1/17		The Batt. moved at 4 p.m. to GOMMECOURT arriving at 11.30 p.m. Four OR's went to hospital and one OR returned. Two OR's went on leave to UK. One OR returned from leave. Lieut. M. C. Barrow at 2nd TOC. 4 F.S.	
GOMMECOURT	18/1/19		The day was spent in inspecting feet and ete. the men were rested.	
			Sergt. JB Delany went to England to take up a commission.	
GOMMECOURT. 29/1/17.		11 a.m.	The Batt. marched to BARASTRE arriving at about 2 p.m. Two OR's went to hospital — one OR returned. Seven OR's returned from leave.	
BARASTRE 30/1/17.			The remainder of day spent in preparing troops into action. The following officers were attached to the Batt. 2nd Lieuts. L.P. Burns, + P.A.M.S.S. (Jesus) Tudor Thomas, John Candy (?) G.E. Morgan, O + Hanson (Ypres). One OR returned from hospital. Ten OR returned from leave.	

WAR DIARY or INTELLIGENCE SUMMARY

Army Form C. 2118.

Place	Date	Hour	Summary of Events and Information	Remarks and references to Appendices
BARASTRE	21/11/17	2 p.m.	We received orders to move forward to ROUGNIES at 11 A.M. and we arrived at 2pm. Company Cmdrs. were moved to reconnoitre route for a further advance to GRAINCOURT and to view the crossing of the Canal. The night of the 21/22nd was spent at DOIGNIES with B.H.Q. in Gen. Pl. men pre-war dugouts. (Tel. a 144). Two OR's returned from Hospital. A draft of 42 OR's from 8th C.T.B.D. — Ten OR's returned from leave.	
DOIGNIES	22/11/17	10.30 p.m.	The Batt. received orders to move forward to GRAINCOURT arriving at 10.30 p.m. The night was spent with 183rd Bde. — BHQ being a junction of Roads to the East of Village. The men being in Pillbill's also to East of the village. (3.1.N.6) Ten OR's returned from leave.	
GRAINCOURT	23/11/17	2.16 A.M.	At 6.10 A.M. the attack was made on BOURLON WOOD by the 186th R.W.F. & 2/5 S.W.B. 2/4th R.W.F. Bn was in Close support & with remainder The 2/4 R.W.F. were under Brigade Reserve. The Infantry was supported by 12 Tanks. At Midday we received orders to move to ANNEUX CHAPELLE B.H.Q. being in a cellar. We arrived under heavy shell fire with a few casualties. "B" & "C" Coys were ordered at 3 p.m. to clear the NORTHERN outskirts of BOURLON WOOD where the attack of the rest of the Brigade was held up.	1 W

WAR DIARY
or
INTELLIGENCE SUMMARY

Army Form C. 2118.

Place	Date	Hour	Summary of Events and Information	Remarks and references to Appendices
	23/10/17 (Continued)		"D" Coy were ordered to make their way up to the left of East Edge of the wood and capture the High Ground N.W. corner of the WOOD overlooking the village of BODELON together with 136 prisoners. The plans hereafter in touch with the Brigade on the left and try a sharp point about 300 yds this side of the Mill stage as soon as the wood —	
			"C" and "B" Companies meanwhile made their way up to what was considered the N.W. corner of the wood. Their advance was marked the right of the N.W. corner of the wood the junction of two rides in the centre of the wood. On J gun rate on the centre of the wood. They came in for heavy M.G. gun and lost many killed and wounded	
			Lieut Col. W.K.G. ONEONE was the O.C. "B" Company was on the — front to them and pressed himself over that "C" Company was to my right and possibly by Detaching Gun fire. Capt. Capt. EWEDWARDS, but was still in furthest progress on Company has been sent forward to the front	
			"B" Company was impossible to be on the right of "C" Company furthest bounded in the J. pattern.	
			A company was at half strength promised a company party of 6d D 14 to the 119 & Brigade M.G. Company. They are kept in reserve during the day but were	

WAR DIARY
or
INTELLIGENCE SUMMARY.
(Erase heading not required.)

Army Form C. 2118.

Place	Date	Hour	Summary of Events and Information	Remarks and references to Appendices
ANNEUX CHAPELLE	24/11/17		Sent up during the night to reinforce a push astray. Counter attack which was expected at day break. Major C.C. Snoding was wounded at 4 a.m. in the afternoon. During the night to reach him we were dug out supplies of ammunition were taken into the firing line. Lieut V.R. returned from leave & took staff duties. Two Companies of the Argylls & Sutherland Highlanders and two coys of Seaforth Highlanders moved into the road between the Martin compound village of the Bois in cover direction of Lieut Col R Buncie. At 9 a.m. this enemy made a counter attack and drove back the Brigade line slightly in the N.W. of G. Sgts M.D.O. "D" Company was able to hold up the attack. On the right Captain R.B. Pascoal was killed by a rifle whilst going round his firing line. The remainder of "C" & "A" Companies under Captain D.P. Scriven were forced to give ground. Others eighth Sands being a 2 Lieut D.P. Laing & Rogers & 2 Lieut Wren were both killed during the morning and 2 Lieut Lee and 2 Lieut Gordon were both wounded and afterwards died of wounds. 2 Lieut L.G. Lemon also 8 Lt also killed during the day. 2 Lieut P.E. Hinsley was wounded during the afternoon.	8 W

WAR DIARY or INTELLIGENCE SUMMARY

Army Form C. 2118.

Place	Date	Hour	Summary of Events and Information	Remarks and references to Appendices
			The position became very uncertain and after dark the different units in the area had become very disorganized, it was too dark to sort them out as much as possible. The different Companies then returned to approx. the same positions as they had on the previous night. During the night of the 24/25th 3 prisoners were sent down by the taking over of the East side of the wood by the 2nd Yorks Fusrs. (2nd Lieut R.F.W. Ruoff and 11 O.R.s assisted to establish from here)	
AVINEUX CHAPELLE	25/11/17		Counter attacks were made by us & still driving the Enemy and taking a number of three ?? Captain S.F. Pearson + Company and 2nd Lieut Toder Thomas (19 R.W.F. attached 18 W.R.) were killed. 2nd Lieut S.R. Penoff was wounded. The SE of the Right front our first line extd near the North Edge of the wood with 'C' Company. Still in position on the left. During the night we were relieved by the 6/9 Division and the batt'n withdrew to the Support line of the HINDENBURG LINE N.W. of HAVRINCOURT. The Batt'n has suffered the following casualties:- 10 Officers and one Warrant Officer killed. Three " and one " " wounded. 136 OR Wounded 126 OR Missing	R.W.

A3634. Wt.W.4973/M687. 750,000 8/16. D.D. & L. Ltd. Forms/C.2118/13.

Army Form C. 2118.

WAR DIARY
or
INTELLIGENCE SUMMARY.
(Erase heading not required.)

Instructions regarding War Diaries and Intelligence Summaries are contained in F. S. Regs., Part II. and the Staff Manual respectively. Title pages will be prepared in manuscript.

Place	Date	Hour	Summary of Events and Information	Remarks and references to Appendices
	25/10/17 (contd)		Two ORs returned from Hospital sick. 9 ORs returned from leave.	
HAVRINCOURT	26/10/17.		The Batt proceeded to LECHELLE where the night was spent. A draft of 36 ORs from IBD arrived. 70 ORs returned from leave.	
LECHELLE	27/10/17.		The Batt received orders to entrain at YTRES at 9 AM for BROOMIES and marched from there to BERLES AU BOIS. 3 ORs returned from leave.	
BERLES AU BOIS	28/10/17.		The day was spent in Batt'n & Coy and reorganizing. The Coy'es were newly but constituted by drafts from LECHELLE. 2 Lieut Robinson taking over B,C & D Coys, 4 Lieut Smith command of A Coy, 2 Lieut W.H.C Creer, C.F Markham and T G White took over B, C, D & D Coys.	
"	29/10/17.		The remainder of the Batt'n kit Balts kit inspected & the making up of deficiency, dept was carried out with Batt'n HQ to Hospital sick. One OR from Hospital. One OR returned from leave.	A.M.

WAR DIARY
or
INTELLIGENCE SUMMARY.

(Erase heading not required.)

Army Form C. 2118.

Place	Date	Hour	Summary of Events and Information	Remarks and references to Appendices
36.R.65.N.80's	30/11/17		All ranks in clubs were shot in and Bivy Alphone parade was made up. Kit left behind at BAR ASTRE was sent for. Captain DR? returned from leave. Men there did no practice during the afternoon.	

Feb 1/1917

Army Form C. 2118.

WAR DIARY
or
INTELLIGENCE SUMMARY.
(Erase heading not required).

War Diary

18th (d). Bn. The Welsh Regiment.

Dec. 1917.

Army Form C. 2118.

WAR DIARY
or
INTELLIGENCE SUMMARY.
(Erase heading not required.)

Instructions regarding War Diaries and Intelligence Summaries are contained in F. S. Regs., Part II. and the Staff Manual respectively. Title pages will be prepared in manuscript.

Place	Date	Hour	Summary of Events and Information	Remarks and references to Appendices
BERLES-AU-BOIS	1st Decr 1917		The Battery employers under orders. 9 guns at 2 hour notice. Bodies were issued to men to ACHIET LE GRT & had were obtained & worked.	OR
			We then received orders to relieve the 167 Bgde. on the night of the 2nd/3rd. One OR to stop the Cook. One OR went on leave. Four OR's were from hospital. Five OR's went to the 4 T.M.B. No.14/13 gate.	A
BERLES-AU-BOIS	2nd Decr 1917		No 193. Regl. J DARNE left camp for Bgde H.Q. The Battery marched from North Road the EQUALLERS and 4th Bgde R.H.A. DYSART CAMP (S.F.B. B) (B.E.S.I.) relieving the relieved the 64th Commissint Bgdes in 16th Susson H.T (Bugani.) The telegrams completed by 4.15.p.m.	A
ERVILLERS	3rd Decr 1917		The day was spent in clearing up the other drill. Lieut L. M. H. Harris was issued on with My OR went to Bgde Hqrs. Four OR's returned from hospital. Four OR's returned from leave. (UK) Staff 11 NCO's arrived from No 6 I.B.D.	OR
ERVILLERS	4th Decr 1917		Orders were received to more to MORY camp at MORY. The more was completed by midday. During the afternoon Pte. and games also some extra drill. 9 OR went on leave to UK. Two men went to hot baths from leave. Two were from Hospital. Three NCOs made reports as machineless to Brigade School also 2 OR for shells. 12 OR to Brigade School. C. 2 OR's attached to W Brigade as Observers.	OR

WAR DIARY
or
INTELLIGENCE SUMMARY
(Erase heading not required.)

Army Form C. 2118.

Place	Date	Hour	Summary of Events and Information	Remarks and references to Appendices
DURROW CAMP MORY.	5/12/17		The Batt. still in Brigade Reserve. Officers and N.C.O's visited the new Brigade front line during the day. Class order ditto. P.B. Bayonet fighting was done. L.M. Gun and sans tactical was carried out and trained. Two OR's returned from leave. 12 OR's went on leave to UK.	
DURROW CAMP MORY	6/12/17		Batt. paraded by Companies during the morning and afternoon. Class and shell P.T + Bayonet fighting was done. The new L.M. Gun and Lewis Gun drill tactics and till was L.M.G was done. The following officers from the 12th Yorks (Pioneers) reported for duty in the line with the Battalion. Lieut C. Mac Donald (attached "A" Coy.) 2nd Lieut J. McGilley (attached "A" Coy) " J. Armstrong (") 2nd Porter ("D" Coy) " J. Kerg (") J.B. Wilson ("D" Coy) 2nd Lieut W.C. ABGH (attached "B" Coy) The Rev. LATOMKIN went on leave to U.K. 17 OR's on leave to UK. Three OR returned from leave. One OR to hospital and one returned from hospital. Captain B.E. Fairbey and 2 OR's returned from U.K. Army Musketry course.	

Army Form C. 2118.

WAR DIARY or INTELLIGENCE SUMMARY

Army Form C. 2118

Place	Date Hour	Summary of Events and Information	Remarks and references to Appendices
DURROW CAMP.	7/12/17. MDRY.	The morning was spent in repeating the drill and close order drill. The Batt. was inspected by the G.O.C. 119th Infantry Brigade at 2.30 p.m. Three O.R's returned from leave. Ten O.R's went on leave to U.K. One O.R went to the 3rd Army Musketry Course MARLOT. One O.R to Hospital. Ten O.R's on Lewis Gun course returned from duty.	
DURROW CAMP.	8/12/17. MDRY.	The Batt. relieved the 17th Batt. in the left front line. The relief was completed by 10.55 p.m. The 17th Welch proceeding into Brigade Reserve. Batt. disp: "A" Company took over the right company front & "B" Company the left company front in TUNNEL TRENCH. "C" Company took over accommodation in support in BURY TRENCH. "D" " " " " " " " Reserve in STRAY Support. Battn. H.Q. in STRAY Support in dug out at V19.c.80.15. The following letter written by Lieut Colonel C.E. PALMER D.S.O. Commanding 119th Brigade R.F.A to BRIGADIER-GENERAL G.B.W. NICHOLSON C.M.G. Commanding 40th Divisional ARTILLERY has been forwarded from 119th BRIGADE H.Q. "To O.C. 119th Infantry Brigade, none can speak too highly — they were magnificent, and I regard it as a very great privilege to have been associated with GENERAL CRAZIER and his gallant Brigade in the glorious affair which presented itself could not be exploited at this time. The results could have been gigantic if steel seen". One wounded from Hospital. Four M.R's Hospital.	

WAR DIARY or INTELLIGENCE SUMMARY

Army Form C. 2118.

Place	Date	Hour	Summary of Events and Information	Remarks and references to Appendices
LEFT Subsector Right Brigade	9/10/17		The day was quiet - weather fast - running. The day was spent in engaging the Sn Equipment and rearranging the ammunition supply. Work was done particularly the front line - improving the posts. Wire (concertina) was erected and wiring squad to work on the wire of the 9th/10th. A draft of 5 B OR's reported from OK.E.I.R.D. Major B.J.B. Coulson assumed Command of the Batt'n. 2 Com OR on leave U.K. Cpl. T. Long returned from 119th Infantry Brigade.	
LEFT Subsector Right Brigade	10/12/17		The unit on the front line was carried on with. Particular attention being given to movement across the river. Loops are being constructed out side the barbed wire that held in to man the post, and the entire held in being reinforced. 2 Com OR's went on leave to U.K.	
LEFT Subsector Right Brigade	11/12/17		From information received an attack was expected on the 11th inst. For this reason Special precautions were taken and everything done to secure the repulse of the enemy. The situation during the night was quiet and no action took place at dawn. Weather slightly colder and colder. Major Barbour with a 2/Lt Davis reported from 5 I.B.D for duty. OK OR/Lt 119th Brigade T/M B Kirkham and man on leave to U.K.	

Major B.J.B. Coulson
Com OR of the 119th Brigade
The D.A.L. 56th FUSILIERS

WAR DIARY or INTELLIGENCE SUMMARY

Army Form C. 2118.

(Erase heading not required.)

Instructions regarding War Diaries and Intelligence Summaries are contained in F. S. Regs., Part II. and the Staff Manual respectively. Title pages will be prepared in manuscript.

Place	Date	Hour	Summary of Events and Information	Remarks and references to Appendices
LEFT SUBSECTR. RIGHT Bgde	12/4/17		An attack was again expected at DAWN and hindering fire was placed out along the front. BARRAGE was opened down at 6.45 A.M. into the Lafayette nation followed by the attack was made to the EAST of BULLECOURT. Heavy gunfire was kept on our right. A German patrol from EAST of BULLECOURT stated that an attack would be made to the WEST of BULLECOURT. 4 O.R's sent to U.K. 1 O.R. to DIVISIONAL STORE ST. LEGER.	
	13/4/17		The enemy put down a GAS BARRAGE on our FRONT LINE, RESERVE and RAILWAY RESERVE between 1 and 2 o'clock in the morning. Two SHELLS which to come over until 10 o'clock. 710 Infantry seven hours fired on Places 56.R on trench to N.K. 1 O.R. wounded. The following joined the battalion. 2/Lt R.W. 29. 2 2/Lt's J.H. H. EDWARDS. A. BARTLETT. G. EVANS. A.E. EDWARDS. H. TUDJ. 3 PRIVATES.	
	14/4/17		The day was quiet. This batch was relieved by the 17 Welsh Regt. at dusk, it's relief being completed at 9.30 P.M. The 18th Welsh were then in BRIGADE RESERVE in RAILWAY RESERVE. The position of Companies at the 9.30 on May ?? POST A + B coy in RAILWAY RESERVE C Coy in RAILWAY EMBANKMENT, H.Q. D Coy 2 platoons 15th L.T.M.B. 2 sections ?? moved the Batta. from the ?? side of PARUR to 857 on their to U.K. 4 O.Rs Joined. 2 wound. 10 R. ??. ?? wounded at dusk 2/Lt ??	
RAILWAY RESERVE	15/4/17		The Battn. had a quiet day and was employed further ?? the 19th the trenches and carrying parties up to the front line. An exercise L-Gun in ?? pointed at ?? for our ??	
	16/4/17		Received orders from 16th Bde to proceed 1 O.R. to ?? 1st 21 R.E. camp right. Enemy trench ?? and ?? to ?? ?? to ?? 4 O.Rs to give the average of Lewis ?? ?? ?? with times. U.K. 1 ?? a Pte ?? la ??. From the Transport ?? 1 Rew 12 ?? Colder, almost a hot day ?? 4 O.Rs on leave to U.K.	

WAR DIARY or INTELLIGENCE SUMMARY

Army Form C. 2118.

Place	Date	Hour	Summary of Events and Information	Remarks and references to Appendices
RAILWAY RES.	17/12/17		Large working parties were sent for consolidating & building communication trenches & their following TRITON and GOLDWING TRENCH. Carrying parties for the 119th MGB and 19th RWF were also provided. Work to improve and add to the accommodation in Company lines was continued. 3 O.R's went on leave U.K. 2nd Lieut O'Salisbury returned from the fourth Army course at FLESCOURT. 2nd Lieut H Jones went sick out to hospital. Casualties Killed - NIL Wounded - O.R.s 4. Died of wounds O.R.'s 1. To UK & O.R. 3. Returned from hospital N.C.O.'s and men with U.B.R.S 1 O.R. to hospitals (Trench Feet)	
	18/12/17		Work as employment as to Bullring continued. Reserve Supplies were received. No working parties for the line were required. RSM Stanley T and 3 other ranks No E.B.D. 10 O.R.s from leave to U.K. to 4 P.O.W. 1 O.R. to hospital. 1 O.R. to hospital 3 O.R's Received 2 O.R's Received to U.K. Joining B.E.F. MGR Lemure Bugler 1.	
	19/12/17			
R.	20/12/17	7.40 p.m.	Battalion in Reserve in MOEUVRES Sept in Left sub-sector at HERMIES Relief complete 7.40 p.m. Dispositions: A Coy - Right front line / TUNNEL TRENCH B do - Left do D do - Support & MG in KITCHENS AVE C do - Reserve - H.Q. in STRAY SUPPORT Batt. H.Q. in STRAY SUPPORT Relieved 1st Bat of 1st Infy & 120th Canadians on relief.	

References - To pages 5,11,8 & 15, Brigade L.M.G. Course 2 to to Brigade Armourers L.M.G. 4 to L.M.G. school LRP LANS 4 OMC Munich L.M.R.

Lieut. Colonel Henry Inf.

WAR DIARY
or
INTELLIGENCE SUMMARY.
(Erase heading not required.)

Army Form C. 2118.

Place	Date	Hour	Summary of Events and Information	Remarks and references to Appendices
CROIX LES SMALL(?)	21/10/17		In the line. Work on Pak on TRITH EL TRENCH. River deep in parts. Communications trenches deep. Misty night this evening.	
	22/10/17		Rest. Reinforcements 3 ORs arrive to U.K. & ORs from leave. 10 ORs taking posts for U.K. Carried parties at night.	
	23/10/17		do. Improvement of trenches and wiring. References 1 OR to Hospital (W), 2 ORs to Hospital (S). 10 ORs leave at 9LR, 10 OR to Brigade School. 9 Camps. Arrivals – 4 OR from U.K.	
			At dawn tunnel trench dug out were evacuated. Bn Hqrs & orders (Transferred) held on Silvania Trail – a A Co's trying line relieved by C & D Co's. & relieved Cos. occupied the dug out of Relief Coy, A & B to come + be accounted to dug outs in Tag alley. Departures 4 OR leave (6 U.K.) 3 OR B Hospital (S) 3 OR from 9OR. Arrivals – 9 OR from School (U.K).	
	24/10/17		Day Normal & Hand had continues – widening + strengthening Park – Improving fire-bays – Reforms recovered the Honor in front of Fag alley – wire – Departures 5 OR in Hospital (U.K.), 16 Hospital (S.), 1 Officer B Hospital school leave (U.K.) Arrivals 1 OR return from leave (U.K.) 2 Lieuts B & C wig assumed duty.	
			(signed) Capt Beltgate Ratree	

WAR DIARY or INTELLIGENCE SUMMARY

Army Form C. 2118.

Place	Date	Hour	Summary of Events and Information	Remarks and references to Appendices
	25-12/17		Reserve Commander Never from Tunnel Trench total 31. + clearing C.T. from Tunnel Trench to Yates J. + 26 - Drilling of dugouts in Bays 15, 17, 19, 22 + 25 - Entrance to Tunnel reinforced following of Trench owing to heavy fall. Patrols active. Departures: 4 O.R. bomb to R.H.Q. Arrivals: 3 O.R. from C.Q.M.S.	
	26/12/17		Inniskillin Camp: The Batt⁰ in the line was relieved by 1/ Welsh + being completed at 7pm - Batches party at 8.40pm - No casualties. The min dug out after hot tea in the line. Work was continued in the various posts running out from Tunnel Trench - The Entrance to the Tunnel were strengthened - Patrols reconnoitred in the night. Casualties: 2 O.R. to Hospital S.I. 2nd Lt S.H.F Edwards to Hospital S.I. Arrivals: 14 O.R. from base (U.K.) 5 O.R. from C.Q.M.S.	
	27/12/17		Inniskillin Camp: The Batt⁰ carried out programme work - J.J. Lt A. Meredith rejoined. Morning Drill - Making Jackets + Breastma & hoganbacks. Departures: 15 O.R. to J. G. Course all Etaques etc, 1 Officer + 2 O.R. to 3rd Army Lewis Gun School (U.K.) Arrivals: 2 O.R. returned from France (U.K.)	

WAR DIARY
or
INTELLIGENCE SUMMARY
(Erase heading not required.)

Army Form C. 2118.

Place	Date	Hour	Summary of Events and Information	Remarks and references to Appendices
Smuts Kamp	28/12/17	—	Programme of work P.T.B. rifle drill under 2/Lieut – making wagons for Gooderm & Christmas boxes. Trees & Xmas dinner was given today event of delinquents. Departures 1. O.R. to Hospital/ Syph Arrivals – 13 African reports from 6/S.A.R.	
	29/12/17		The Ball. Moved Camp from Smutskloll to Wortkamp of diary which had just been evacuated by 10. S.A.I.R. P.T. & B. Gooders Christmas boxes made (wagonloads) headbands – firing aids – Departures 2. O.R. to Smutskloll Come Styfle Arrivals 13 O.R. from (eant.U.R.) 2. O.R. to Hospital (S)	
Wortkamp	30/12/17		Making Gooder Christmas program (wagon load) Guard for Bwa N.S.L 2.1/6.R 6 to 8 Parade 2.10 a.m. Departures:- 4 O.R. to E1 Cape School on Course. 5 O.R. from leave (U.K.) 1 O.R. from E1 Caps School on Course Arrivals:- 2 O.R. from 4.0 D D.W. Dept Coll	
			Ball'n Parade + Inspection – making Gooder & Christmas rolls Departures 5 O.R. on leave (U.K.) 1 to Hospital (S) Arrivals 3 O.R. refund from leave (U.R.)	
	31/12/17		Fraaug hand – made for E4p —	

Thomas Clinch Lt
OC Detachment

Army Form C. 2118.

WAR DIARY
or
INTELLIGENCE SUMMARY.
(Erase heading not required.)

War Diary
18th Bn. Welsh Regt.
January 1918

WAR DIARY
or
INTELLIGENCE SUMMARY.
(Erase heading not required.)

Army Form C. 2118.

Place	Date	Hour	Summary of Events and Information	Remarks and references to Appendices
Warloy	1.11.18 morn		The Battⁿ returned to 11.½ line at dusk relief was complete at 5.30 a.m. the position of Bns was as follows: a Coy at front "B" Coy on left front in support "C" Coy at Reserve DCC. Departures: 7 O.Rs on leave (to U.K.) Arrivals: a/Capt C.E. Markham from leave (U.K.) 2 O.Rs to Hospital (sick) 3 O.Rs from leave (U.K.) 1 O.N.C. to DADOS 10th Div for instructions on uniforms ormarees. The Battn carried out training programme in the morning — P.D. + close order drill — to B.P. in wg/s above & sunny bags.	
			Military Honours: The Field Marshal Commanding in Chief has awarded the following distinguished service order to undermentioned 25/3/17 + Capt F. M. Mathews 1st(S) Battn 10th(S) Battn Welsh Regt The Military Cross 27/10/17 2ⁿᵈ Lt J.P. J.R.W. May The Distinguished Conduct Medal No 278/77 Sgt M. Bowen " A.J. Lawrence 28/1/12	

WAR DIARY or INTELLIGENCE SUMMARY

Army Form C. 2118.

Place	Date	Hour	Summary of Events and Information	Remarks and references to Appendices
	1/1/18		Military Honors (Cont'd). (Official notice from H.Q. 40 Divn on to O/C 119 Infantry Brigade dated 29/12/17.) The IV Corps Commander under authority of His Majesty awarded the Military Medal to the U/M NCOs and men as under:— Bar to Military Medal 28203 Sgt (A/C.S.M.) W. Burns 18/B⁺ Welsh Regiment The Military Medal 53390 Cpl G. Evans 18 B⁺ Welsh Regiment Also 28674 Pte I. Libby 156 B/139³ 28580 Sgt M. Newman " " 283 25 do J.I. Jones Min. Reg⁺ 28670 Rfle G.I. Handy " " 275 04 Cpl J.J. Foulk " " 28704 Rfle I. Jarry " " 28268 Pte W. Williams " " 281731 Cpl J. McBarley " " 277 87 Sgt R. Thomas 211489 do H. Miller " " 382 512 Sgt E.G. Wyatt 512 23 Pte A. Lobgett The congratulations of the Commanding Officer of the Batt⁺ were conveyed to the Recipients together with those of the G.O.C. 9/16 119th Infantry Brigade, the Divisional Commander of the 40th Divn⁺ & the Army Commander in the field.	

WAR DIARY
or
INTELLIGENCE SUMMARY.
(Erase heading not required.)

Army Form C. 2118.

Place	Date	Hour	Summary of Events and Information	Remarks and references to Appendices
IN THE FIELD	2/1/17		In the Field. Working parties constructing Machine + Lewis Gun Pits in consequence of Evacuation of Tunnel front Dug out. — C.I.O. treating trench in Bolsdrenshard and refrained. — Shells & rained + improved — 2 Nurses approached from front line. Departures: 21st Hospital (S). Arrivals: 6 O.R. from Leave (UK) 7 on leave to (UK) L⁺ Lawrence L⁺ Roberts + 3 × 2 L⁺ Rank	
	3/1/17		Enemy Artillery active Minerva guns shells the back across Minerva guns — 77.8 shells at Junction Mulga & the front. Shells the back across Minerva quad. — Our Artillery active. — Construction on of Shelter in Bow Lane with R.E. — Gas cavalry patrol from fire for 30yds. clearing up OP leading to hers 2,6. 9,10 10,15 — Patrol went to wind out at 5 ft at midnight — 2 men taken wind out from C.P. front during stand to until Stand down in the morning. — Knocking of the artillery on our + enemy Side — Front line + Bonlane was shelled — (B⁺) Winning party held 60 enemy trench across FAG Alley. Departures: 5 O.R. to Hospital (S). 7 O.R. Leave (UK) 1 O.R. Killen Layton " L⁺ a Cop⁺ 7 O. Rankes S. Arrivals. 3 O.R. from Linden (UK)	
	4/1/17		Construction of Shelter under R.E. — " Supplies 10 hours parties + light patrols went not at 5pm and holding line and reconnoitring Evacuating front of trust. — Our artillery fairly active. Silence order to be carried out. In journey Departures: 7 O.R. Leave to U.K. Arrivals 1 O.R. from Hospital 4 O.R. to Hospital sick 7 O.R. from Leave 2 O.R. to Hospital wounded 1 O.R. Killed in action	
	5/1/17		The M⁹ Battn relieved by advised this Battn, relieved and billets in Huntsville by P.30 hrs. The Norton L Corps was to follow M⁰ M⁰ Norton to follow Man⁰ Road, L.C. RAILWAY EMBANKMENT + Bull RAILWAY RAVINE, MARY JANE RAILWAY BEFORE Leslie by 8 Gardner ref from Camp Arrivals. - 5 O.R. from Leave Extsa 7 O.R. to Ripon sick 2 2⁺ Linholl returned from leave 7 O.R. to Hospital sick 4 O.R. ret⁺ from Leave 1 " Dismount	

WAR DIARY
or
INTELLIGENCE SUMMARY.
(Erase heading not required.)

Army Form C. 2118.

Place	Date	Hour	Summary of Events and Information	Remarks and references to Appendices
Dr Suffolk Railway Reserve	6/1/18		Working parties were detailed for work on Gun boot store (Railway Reserve); A.9 Coy in B.11 Coy TRENCH; Construction of strong point in MARS LANE; Billet construction on Left Batt's front. Departures. 7 O.R's on Leave. Arrivals. 3 O.R's from Leave. 1 " to Stopster sch. 1 " to J.R.I. 2 " on Sanitary Course.	
"	7/1/18		During the afternoon the enemy trench mortared about 9 shells round by the 121 Brigade. Working Parties of 200 O.R's on all un-athletics for work at different points on the Brigade front. At 4:30 p.m. an O. Hand with artillery support supported the Enemy from the 121 Rifle Brigade line. Departure. 7 O.R's on Leave. Arrivals. 2 O.R's from Leave 2 " to hospital with 5 " " J.R.I. 20 " on Course at B. course at staple actions 2 " " Stopster	
"	8/1/18		Working Parties went out to work with the supervision of the R.E's on the Bypass limit. The day was quiet. Weather colder. Departures. 7 O.R's on Leave Arrivals. 5 O.R's from Leave 1 " " hospital.	

WAR DIARY
or
INTELLIGENCE SUMMARY
(Erase heading not required.)

Army Form C. 2118

Instructions regarding War Diaries and Intelligence Summaries are contained in F. S. Regs., Part II. and the Staff Manual respectively. Title Pages will be prepared in manuscript.

Place	Date	Hour	Summary of Events and Information	Remarks and references to Appendices
RAILWAY RESERVE	9-1-18		Working parties were out to left and rear of the Brigade front. At night this Battalion relieved the 17th Welch Regt in the left sub-sector. Rifle Butts & RAILWAY SUPPORT. "A" Coy RIGHT FRONT Coy. "B" Coy LEFT FRONT Coy. "C" RESERVE Coy STRAY SUPPORT. "D" SUPPORT Coy KNUCKLE AVENUE. The day was quiet. Weather snowy. Departures 2 O.R's on leave 2 " to Hospital sick Arrivals 5 from leave 10 " Rgtl school.	
Left Subsector Left Brigade	10/1/18		The day was quiet. Our Patrol encountered a hostile patrol and a sharp exchange of rifle fire ensued. Smoke patrol was placed in NO MANS LAND during the hours of darkness and particular precautions were taken at dawn in view of a statement made by a prisoner that regards an attack. Departures 7 O.R's on leave. 2 to Hospital sick Lieut. Loftus (M.O.R.C.) admitted to F.A.	Arrival 5 O.R's from LOB 1 " Hospital 1 " leave. Lieut. was Battigate reposed from leave.
	11/1/18		Snow and some rain. The risks of the trenches were very bad on features. The Batt'n did as a company relief. "B" coy to left and "C" to the right front. "A" coy into Reserve and "B" coy into Support. at 10 pm. Our artillery wired over gas shells came flashing artillery work. All men were put to work on the baling out and pumping water from the front line trenches. Departures 7 O.R's in leave & sick 1 " to Hospital sick	Arrivals 5 O.R's from leave

WAR DIARY
or
INTELLIGENCE SUMMARY
(Erase heading not required.)

Army Form C.2118

Place	Date	Hour	Summary of Events and Information	Remarks and references to Appendices
Left Schreiberhof Left Rouges	12/1/18		Thaw continues. Special precautions are still being taken in view of possible attack. Enemy Artillery fire showed the day was very quiet. Work repairing the damage done by the thaw. Arrival. Capt. J.A. Wells (M.C) Departure 2 O.R's to Hospital sick 4 O.R's returned from leave. 3 " called in Action 3 " Hospital wounded 7 " on leave to U.K.	
	13/1/18		Weather cold again. The Batt. was relieved by the 17th Welch – relief being completed at 9.15 pm. The Batt. moved into Reserve at "NORTH CAMP MOER". Arrival. 4 O.R's returned from D Corps adre. Departures 1 O.R. on leave to U.K. , 1 " , 8HQ CETOQUET. 3 " to Hospital sick	
	14/1/18		The day was spent in cleaning up and reorganising the men. The Batt's billeted at the 9m O.R.Y Batt. Camp. Improvements were continued with. Arrival. 2 O.R's from Convalescence Camp Hospital Departure 2 O.R's on leave to U.K. 7 " " Hospital sick 4 " " "	

WAR DIARY
or
INTELLIGENCE SUMMARY.
(Erase heading not required.)

Army Form C. 2118.

Instructions regarding War Diaries and Intelligence Summaries are contained in F. S. Regs., Part II. and the Staff Manual respectively. Title pages will be prepared in manuscript.

Place	Date	Hour	Summary of Events and Information	Remarks and references to Appendices
NORTH CAMP MORL	15/10/18		Batt⁰ in reserve. Owing to thaw and heavy rain the state of the ground becoming very bad. The Batt⁰ used for working parties in and round the Camp. A Coy shoot on the Rifle Range. Departures 4 O.R's to Hospital sick. Arrivals 4 O.R's from leave. 9 " on leave to U.K.	
	16/10/18		Work in the camp continued with Companies held Kit inspections. Special attention being given to providing such men with three pairs of socks. Weather continues to be very bad. Departures 4/Lt Col R.M.D. Gordon to Hospital sick. 7 O.R's on leave to U.K.	Arrivals. 3 officers from I.B.D. 1 O.R. from I.B.D. 4 " " leave.
	17/10/18		Batt⁰ received foot treatment at MORL. Batt⁰ relieved the 17th Welsh in the Left Sub Sector Left Brigade Front. Owing to the bad state of the trenches the front line Companies (A&B) marched out at 2p.m. so as to be at PORTERS DUMP before dusk. The relief was completed by 8.15. "A" Coy Right Front. "B" Coy Left Front. "C" Coy Support. D Coy Reserve.	

Wt. W4973/M687. 750,000. 8/16. D. D. & L. Ltd. Forms/C.2118/13.

WAR DIARY
or
INTELLIGENCE SUMMARY.
(Erase heading not required.)

Army Form C. 2118.

Place	Date	Hour	Summary of Events and Information	Remarks and references to Appendices
	17/1/18	continued	Owing to the difficulty of communication each man took in two clean rations. Special precautions were taken with regard to care of feet. Extra socks were arranged for and a scheme by which dry socks will be given to each man in reserve daily has been arranged. Departures. Arrivals. 10 O.R. from hospital. 6 O.R. on one hour. 4 " to Hospital (S) 1 " " Wounded.	
STRAY SUPPORT. Left Sub-Sector. Left Brigade.	18/1/18		Weather still bad. All communication trenches blocked. Ranks now the B.T. have been marked out for ration parties. The B.T. use by night. Ranks have also been marked out to enable ration to be taken up to company dumps by mules. The day was quiet. Very little rain fell. Departures. Arrivals. 20 O.R. from leave. 2 O.R. to Hospital sick. 5 " on leave to U.K.	
STRAY SUPPORT. Left Sub-Sector. Left Brigade.	19/1/18.		No rain has fallen during the last 24 hours. The work on the B.T. is being pressed on with. Rations were brought up on mules direct to the Rifles Coy — the remainder being dumped at B.H.Q. and carried up by ration parties. Inter Company relief carried out. Left Front. "A" Coy. Right Front "C" Coy. Support "A" Coy. Reserve "B" Coy.	

WAR DIARY
or
INTELLIGENCE SUMMARY.
(Erase heading not required.)

Army Form C. 2118.

Place	Date	Hour	Summary of Events and Information	Remarks and references to Appendices
	19/1/18.	continued.	Departures. Arrivals 90 O.R.s from leave.	
20/1/18. STRAY SUPPORT Left Section Left Brigade			2 O.R.s to hospital sick. 3 " on leave. 1 " on police convoy. Dept. O.Rs going on leave & not return. Weather improving. Work of cleaning and pumping continued in Support and Reserve Companies worked on the Support line. Carrying Coys worked on the tunnel trench. C.T. still impassable for large trains of trolleys. Front line hot post carried & the front line by night are the top. Departures. Arrivals. 13 O.R.s from leave. 6 O.R.s on leave to rest. 2 " J.R.O. Canada. 7 " to hospital sick. 50 " Reinforcing draft from [?]	
24/1/18 STRAY SUPPORT			Slight fall of rain. Work on the improvement of trenches continued with The Batt.s were relieved by the 17th Welsh and at 6.45 p.m. came into Brigade support at RAILWAY RESERVE. A Coy Bn. Support "C" Coy in RAILWAY EMBANKMENT "B" & "D" RAILWAY RESERVE. Departures. Arrivals. 9 O.R.s from leave. 1 O.R. Divisional P. Staff. 1 " hospital sick. 5 " on leave to rest.	

Army Form C. 2118.

WAR DIARY
or
INTELLIGENCE SUMMARY.
(Erase heading not required.)

Instructions regarding War Diaries and Intelligence Summaries are contained in F. S. Regs., Part II. and the Staff Manual respectively. Title pages will be prepared in manuscript.

Place	Date	Hour	Summary of Events and Information	Remarks and references to Appendices
RAILWAY RESERVE Brigade Support	22/1/18		The Batt^s provided working parties under R.E. arrangements in the communication trenches on the Brigade FRONT. The work of salvage and clearing up of Railway Reserve Lines were renewed in the Company Lines and other improvements made. Two Companies attended the Foot Baths at St Lager. Departures. 5 to Hospital sick. Arrivals. 1 O.R. from leave. 5 on leave to UK.	
	23/1/18		R.E. Working parties were provided on C.T's. Work in the Batt^n area was continued. Weather improving. Departures 1st to Hospital sick 3 O.R. " " " on leave to UK. Arrival 5 O.R. from leave 2 " " Hospital	
	24/1/18.		B Two Companies had the Foot Baths at St Lager. R.E. Working Parties were provided and the work on Batt & Lines continued with. Departures 2 to Hospital sick 8 O.R. on leave to UK. Arrivals. 3 O.R. from Hospital 11 " " Leave.	

WAR DIARY or INTELLIGENCE SUMMARY

Army Form C. 2118.

Place	Date	Hour	Summary of Events and Information	Remarks and references to Appendices
RAILWAY RESERVE Brigade Support.	25th January 1918.		Working party (full strength) was provided during the morning. "A" & "B" Companies attended the foot drill. RAILWAY RESERVE during the afternoon. This Batt'n relieved the 17th Welch in the front line left sub sector left Brigade on the evening of the 25/1/18. "A" Coy on the Front Right Coy. "B" Coy on the left Front Coy. "9" Coy in Support (BERG TRENCH.) & "C" in Reserve (SPRAY SUPPORT) The relief was completed by 6.30 p.m. The trenches were much wetter. The weather had been dry for the last few days. The Brigade on our left were raiders. Departures. Arrival. 5 O.R's on leave to U.K. 1 " " " to hospital	50 R. on leave to U.K. + O.R's from I.B.D.
SPRAY SUPPORT. Left sub sector Left Brigade	26th January 1918.		The front line Companies worked in their front and on the TUNNEL TRENCH. The Support Company worked on BERG between KNOCKIE and BOW LANE. The Reserve Company spent the after in bringing up R.E. material for improving and revetting the trenches. Major G.S. Gordon 12'R.S.U.B. joined the Batt'n as second in command officer. Departures. Arrival. 1 W.O. took sick 8 O.R's returned from leave 6 O.R's on leave Kent.	

Army Form C. 2118.

WAR DIARY
or
INTELLIGENCE SUMMARY.
(Erase heading not required.)

Instructions regarding War Diaries and Intelligence Summaries are contained in F.S. Regs., Part II. and the Staff Manual respectively. Title pages will be prepared in manuscript.

Place	Date	Hour	Summary of Events and Information	Remarks and references to Appendices
STRAY SUPPORT Left Subsector Left Brigade	27/1/16		A very quiet day. The C. Trans were quite open to traffic in this sector. Captain L.J.A. Will M.C. left the Batt.n for 5th Brigade to take over the duties of Brigade major. Work was continued in Burg Trench and also on the position the front line. Light gun latrines were made. Roth Company relief took place. "C" Coy relieved "A" Coy Front line — "A" Coy to Reserve "D" " " " " " "B" " "Left" " — "B" " a Support. Departures. 5 O.R's on leave to U.K.	Arrivals. 5 O.R's returned from leave "2" " " " Hospital
Left Subsector Left Brigade	28/1/18		A very quiet day. Enemy Aeroplanes active by night (full moon.) The state of "no mans land" is very much improved and no patrols have been able to move about with greater ease than previously. On account of the dry weather, better progress has been made with the repairs to the trenches. Departures. 2 O.R's to Hospital sick. 6 " on leave to U.K.	Arrivals. Lieut. M. H. B. O'R. joining 3rd Durham L.I. from 35th D.R.D. " 3 O.R's joined " " " " 3 " " " under here

Army Form C. 2118.

WAR DIARY
or
INTELLIGENCE SUMMARY.
(Erase heading not required.)

Instructions regarding War Diaries and Intelligence Summaries are contained in F. S. Regs., Part II. and the Staff Manual respectively. Title pages will be prepared in manuscript.

Place	Date	Hour	Summary of Events and Information	Remarks and references to Appendices
BRAY SUPPORT Lt Col Puch Left Brigade	29/1/18		Work was continued on BURY TRENCH and also on the posts in the front line. The day was very fine and the Training Ground. Hostile aeroplanes dropped a number of bombs on roads near MORY. The 2/8th Batt Welsh were relieved by the 17th Welsh + relief complete by 7.30 pm. The Battn went into Brigade Reserve at NORTHAMPTON MORY. Arrivals 16 O.R's from leave	Departures 5 Off's + Sgt + 6 O.R. 5 to Hospl Wounded
NORTH CAMP MORY	30/1/18		The Battn relieved by Companies. The day was spent in having kit inspections and generally cleaning up. The men were paid. Work about the camp was continued with. Arrivals Lt Col G.H. Gaiger from 2 Ranker classes 2 O.R from leave 1 from Hospital	Departures 5 O.R's on leave to U.K.
NORTH CAMP MORY	31/1/18		Snow. Close colder. Drill was done and a large working party of 200 men supplied to the R.E's for night work. The work of improving the Camp was continued with. Arrivals 6 O.R 2 from leave, 1 from Camp 3 from Hospl	Departures 5 O.R's on leave to U.K.

C.E. Gaiger Major Comdg 17th Batt S. Wales B

A 8834 Wt.W4973/M687 750,000 8/16 D.D. & L. Ltd. Forms/C.2118/13

Army Form C. 2118.

WAR DIARY
or
INTELLIGENCE SUMMARY.
(Erase heading not required.)

Vol 21

War Diary

February 1918

18th Welsh Regt.

WAR DIARY
or
INTELLIGENCE SUMMARY.

Army Form C. 2118.

Place	Date	Hour	Summary of Events and Information	Remarks and references to Appendices
NORTH CAMP MORY	1/2/19		Two Companies and the draft were put on hauling down the marquee. The other two companies worked on the arrangement of huts and general improvement of the camp. — 400 duck boards were changed. The time at fires. The wiring guard made conveniences which were erected by C Coy. Circus at night. Departures: [illegible]	Arrivals: [illegible]
"	2/2/16		The four companies and B.H.Q. attended the foot contest at ERVILLERS during the morning. The Batt. returned to the 19th [illegible] the Left Sub Sector Left Anges. Relief complete by 7.00. [illegible]	Arrivals: [illegible]

WAR DIARY
or
INTELLIGENCE SUMMARY.
(Erase heading not required.)

Army Form C. 2118.

Place	Date	Hour	Summary of Events and Information	Remarks and references to Appendices
STRAY SUPPORT LEFT Subsector for Brigade.	3/2/18.		The Batt. in the Line — "A" and "B" Coys in the Front Line. "C" in Support "B" Coy in Reserve. "A" & "B" Coys in were on the posts in the front line. "C" in Supp. Trench and BAUMANS LOOP. "B" in TUNNEL TRENCH and far to provide supply parties for the RE material required by the Batt. The usual patrols were sent out during the night. The state of no man's land never improved measurably preventing Pat. from placing out wire. The right SNIPERS went out to ARGENTINES by day. Wiring carried out. Trench bridges Capt. QUILTER and 2/Lt Lewis returning. Officers Made. 2 Platoon 6 OR "A" in dent.	
"	4/2/18.		Work was continued with as done. The trench is much slipped when the day sun can be gots. Patrols went out to get posts improvements Kept up. taken. Continued daring might Recent comp.in shell fire which shewed a large amount of shelling and to shorten large fires in enemy lines to the outskirts of BAMAL on the outskirts of BAMAL Our Artillery. Trench Mortars are in life. heavy fires on the outskirts of BAMAL. Dispositions. 5 O.R's in canteen for " 10 " " E.F. R.?	3 O.R.'s per leave.

WAR DIARY
or
INTELLIGENCE SUMMARY.

Army Form C. 2118.

Place	Date	Hour	Summary of Events and Information	Remarks and references to Appendices
STRAW SUPPORT	5/9/16		The work in the front line and BURG TRENCH was continued with. BURG TRENCH is now in good condition. BOWMAN'S LOBB (view L.H. Coy H.Q.) Inter Company relief "C" Coy relieved "A" Coy on the right and "B" Coy relieved "D" Coy on the left company front. In accordance with the alteration in the Brigade two hundred men of the 17th Welsh with ten Officers was posted to this Unit. One hundred men and two Officers reported for duty. Arrivals.	2 9th tonight via 3 RO in Line Departures 10 R to Hospital 5 " on Leave
"	6/9/16		Arrivals: B.G. Bowman 30 O.R. from train 30 O.R. from Hospital. A view of the weakness of the Battn. in support R.E. working parties usually supplied by support when sufficiently fit. The trenches are in very much condition the weather remains good. Arrivals. 5 O.R. arrived from leave	Departures 10 R to Hospital 5 " on Leave
"	7/9/16		The firm have been quiet up to the present. No Infantry action on this front. Work proceeded with Arrivals. 10 O.R. from Hospital 3 " " leave	Departures 20 R to Hospital exit

Army Form C. 2118.

WAR DIARY
or
INTELLIGENCE SUMMARY.
(Erase heading not required.)

Instructions regarding War Diaries and Intelligence Summaries are contained in F. S. Regs., Part II. and the Staff Manual respectively. Title pages will be prepared in manuscript.

Place	Date	Hour	Summary of Events and Information	Remarks and references to Appendices
RAILWAY RESERVE	8/3/18		The Battⁿ was relieved by the 21st Middlesex and returned to Brigade Reserve in Railway Reserve. Working Parties were sent daily to work in the front line with another party pushing up RE material from Ecoust Dump. Arrivals. 5 O.R.'s from base. 3 " " JIAD	Departures. 5 O.R.'s to base. 3 " to Hospital. etc.
	9/3/18		The usual daily working parties in the front line during the day were found by this Battⁿ. Other work was done as the lines & Billets in preparation for the Divisional Relief.	Departures. 7 O.R.'s to base. Arrivals. #O.R. from hospital.
	10/3/18		The weather continues fine and a great deal of work has been done in connection to the trenches. R.E. working parties as usual. Arrivals. 6 O.R.'s from base.	Departures. 5 O.R.'s on leave. 4 hospital. 2nd etc.

Place	Date	Hour	Summary of Events and Information	Remarks and references to Appendices
DURHAM CAMP. No 2.	11/2/16		The Batt: was retired by daylight by the 9/5 & 7/6 Sherwood Foresters. The 9/5 - S.F. relieved "C" Coy in MANSORSAST and "B" Coy in RAILWAY RESERVE. The 7/6 "B" Coy in RAILWAY RESERVE and Fort 57 Q. Relief was Complete by 1.30 P.M. "A" Coy was not relieved. The Transport remained at BELFAST CAMP. EQUILLERS. Arrived. Departures. 2. O.R. from Hospital 2. O.R. to Hospital on leave	
	12/2/16		The day was devoted to cleaning up and refitting. Murner, Ed Luttrell took over inspector and the necessary in dark part on. Agreeably to W.O. "T" 90 OR was transfered to the RTO BOISLEUX AU MONT. This guard will be relieved on the 14/2/16. Transport Guard to York Camp MERCATEL. Arrived. Departures. 5 O.R. on leave	

WAR DIARY
or
INTELLIGENCE SUMMARY.

Army Form C. 2118.

Place	Date	Hour	Summary of Events and Information	Remarks and references to Appendices
DURHAM CAMP No 2	13/2/18		A programme of training including Musketry, Trench Repair, Rifle Exercise, Drill (Drilling in to the Army) was commenced. A Class for junior NCOs was started in charge of the RSM. Foot ball during the afternoon. A Concert was given to the men during the evening. There was no parade in the Bn Rs.	
			Arrivals. 9 O.Rs from leave. 2nd Lt W. Brown from I.B.D.	
			Departures 5 O.R's to [?] 2. [?] to [?]	
"	14/2/18		Training during the morning. Football during the other noon. The Battn was paid. Church service. Bath Parade at 12 noon.	
			Arrivals	
			Departures 7 O.R's to [?] 2 [?] to [?]	

Army Form C. 2118.

WAR DIARY
or
INTELLIGENCE SUMMARY.
(Erase heading not required.)

Instructions regarding War Diaries and Intelligence Summaries are contained in F. S. Regs., Part II. and the Staff Manual respectively. Title pages will be prepared in manuscript.

Place	Date	Hour	Summary of Events and Information	Remarks and references to Appendices
DURHAM CAMP No 2	15/2/18		The Battalion carried on with the programme of training during the morning. During the afternoon inter-company football matches were played. Arrivals :- 2 or from MGB Departures :- 1 2nd Lt S Lyon 7 or 6/7/9 to G.C.	
	16/2/18		A & B. Coys. bathed at MERCATEL in the morning and continued with the programme of training in the afternoon. C & D. Coys continued with the programme of training during the morning and bathed at MERCATEL in the afternoon. The Commanding Officer, 16 other officers & 20 NCOs attended a lecture on "Intelligence" at the BOISLEUX THEATRE at 5 p.m. Arrival :- Departures :- 6 2nd Lt W Cleave M.G.C. 2nd Lt F Little M.G.C.	

Army Form C. 2118.

WAR DIARY
or
INTELLIGENCE SUMMARY.
(Erase heading not required.)

Place	Date	Hour	Summary of Events and Information	Remarks and references to Appendices
DURHAM. CAMP No 2.	17/2/18		Church Parade was held at 10.30 A.M. At 4.30 p.m. a working party of 18 Officers 600 O.R. left the camp by light railway for WANCOURT to work on the Corps line of entrenchments. The party returned to camp at 12 midnight. Arrivals. 9 E.R. from Leave. 2 Offrs 200 O.R. from France. Departures. D/Instons O.C in Camp	
	18/2/18		No training was carried out during the morning. Working parties were found to improve the rifle range near camp and to build revetments round the huts in the camp. In the afternoon inter-company football matches were played. Five officers went to reconnoitre the ground to the Left & Centre Brigades of the 3rd Division.	

Army Form C. 2118.

WAR DIARY
or
INTELLIGENCE SUMMARY.
(Erase heading not required.)

Place	Date	Hour	Summary of Events and Information	Remarks and references to Appendices
DURHAM NO 2 CAMP.	18/2/18		(Cont'd) Arrivals. Major Stratton, 2/Lt. Bowman, 2/Lt. O.S. Moore, 2/Lt. N.J. Brinkley } from I.B.D. Departures. 6 o.r. relief.	
	19/2/18.		The programme of training was carried out with during the morning. Some officers reconnoitred the ground to the Right Brigade 3rd Division. Battalion Sports were held during the afternoon and Coy Kitchen trade place in the evening. Arrivals 2 o.r. from NOYELLES Departures. 7 o.r. relief. 2 o.r. sick	

Army Form C. 2118.

WAR DIARY
or
INTELLIGENCE SUMMARY.
(Erase heading not required.)

Instructions regarding War Diaries and Intelligence Summaries are contained in F. S. Regs., Part II. and the Staff Manual respectively. Title pages will be prepared in manuscript.

Place	Date	Hour	Summary of Events and Information	Remarks and references to Appendices
DURHAM CAMP.	20/2/18		The programme of Training was continued with during the morning. In the evening the Battalion went up to WANCOURT dug light railway, extending at 5pm, which was carried out on the Corps Defence line, excavating & wiring. The last party returned to camp at 12 midnight. Departures 1 /2/Lt Jeans 1 Lieut F. Hicks Arrivals 5 O.R. from Base 1 O.R. from Hospital 8 O.R. from Leave	
	21/2/18		The Battalion moved from DURHAM CAMP to 11 a.m. arriving in No. 2 CAMP BLAIRVILLE at 1.30 p.m. No 2 Camp was taken over from the 14th H.L.I. Arrivals 4 O.R. from Leave Lt. W.R. Finn Gordon Departures 1 /2/Lt Jeans 2 O.R. to N.R.A.	

Army Form C. 2118.

WAR DIARY
or
INTELLIGENCE SUMMARY.
(Erase heading not required.)

Place	Date	Hour	Summary of Events and Information	Remarks and references to Appendices
No 2 Camp BLAIRVILLE	22/2/18		The programme of training was continued with during the morning. A & B Coys trained in BLAIRVILLE in the morning & C & D in the afternoon. The Battalion football team played a team from the 13th Field Ambulance. Orderlies 2 o.r. from Leave 2 o.r. from M.S. Departures 2 o.r. to Leave 3 o.r. to M.S. Hospital	
	23/2/18		The 119th Brigade was inspected by the Brigadier General on the parade ground in No 3 Camp at 11 A.M. The Brigade marched past in column of companies. The 18th Welch Band was on parade. Inter-company football matches were played in the afternoon. Arrivals 8 o.r. from leave	Departures 7 o.r. to Leave 1 M + 1 o.r. to Course

Army Form C. 2118.

WAR DIARY
or
INTELLIGENCE SUMMARY.
(Erase heading not required.)

Place	Date	Hour	Summary of Events and Information	Remarks and references to Appendices
No 2 Camp BLAIRVILLE	24/2/18		Church parade was held at 11AM. The Commanding Officer, Adjutant & Company Commanders reconnoitred the line around WANCOURT starting from camp at 9.30 AM and returning at 2 pm. The Battalion Rugby team played a team of Corps Distillerymen in the afternoon. Major Spargo arrived in the evening & took command of the Battalion. Departures:— 1 O in at ease 2 " from HQ. Arrivals:— Off 1 O in at ease from Leave 3 " from HQ	

WAR DIARY or INTELLIGENCE SUMMARY

Army Form C. 2118.

Place	Date	Hour	Summary of Events and Information	Remarks and references to Appendices
BLAIRVILLE CAMP.	25/9/18		Training was carried on according to the Battalion programme from 8.30 A.M. to 12.30 P.M. and from 1.30 P.M. to 3 P.M. A Coy. held firing practice on the range from 9 A.M. to 11 A.M. & D. Coy. from 11.30 A.M. to 12.30 P.M. and 1.30 to 3.30 P.M. Arrivals:- 8 O.R. from Base 3 " MGS 2 " " Bomber	Officers:- 6 O.R. from Base 1 " at X Base
	26/9/18		Training was carried on from 8.30 A.M. to 12.30 P.M. & 1.30 P.M. to 4 P.M. C & D. Coys used the rifle range in the morning. At 1.30 P.M. the Battalion paraded under Major Gough and carried out a practice "Counter Attack". The objective was a trench near the FICHEUX ROAD. The Battalion advanced over a distance of 1000 yards, deploying into artillery formation & then extended order when under effective rifle fire.	3 " " " Base 5 " " " "

Army Form C. 2118.

WAR DIARY
or
INTELLIGENCE SUMMARY.
(Erase heading not required.)

Place	Date	Hour	Summary of Events and Information	Remarks and references to Appendices
BLAIRVILLE CAMP	27/2/18		The Battalion paraded at 8.30 A.M. under Major Forsyth. A "practice" counter attack was carried out over the same ground as on the previous day. The General Officer Commanding in Chief watched the operations from the FICHEUX ROAD. Training was carried on under Company arrangements from 1.30 P.M. to 3 P.M. Strength:— Officers 8 on parade, 3 on leave, 1 H.Q.P. O.R.s — on leave, on course, on H.Q.P., on Command.	

Army Form C. 2118.

WAR DIARY
or
INTELLIGENCE SUMMARY.
(Erase heading not required.)

Place	Date	Hour	Summary of Events and Information	Remarks and references to Appendices
No 2 Camp BLAIRVILLE	28/9/18		The Battalion marched from BLAIRVILLE to GOUY EN ARTOIS, starting from BLAIRVILLE at 9 AM and arriving in GOUY at 11.30 AM, where they were billeted. The route was via RANSART, BEAUMETZ & MONCHIET. Strength — 9 officers 3 r.mar Arrival — 6 ... r.mar 2 ... r.mar 3 ... 10th 5 ... r 13th 118	H M Keogh Major Commanding 1st Manchesters

40th Division.
119th Infantry Brigade.

WAR DIARY

18th BATTALION

THE WELCH REGIMENT

MARCH 1918

WAR DIARY
or
INTELLIGENCE SUMMARY

Army Form C. 2118.

15 Welsh Regt

WAR DIARY
FOR
MARCH 1918.

WAR DIARY or INTELLIGENCE SUMMARY

(Erase heading not required.)

Army Form C. 2118.

Instructions regarding War Diaries and Intelligence Summaries are contained in F. S. Regs., Part II. and the Staff Manual respectively. Title pages will be prepared in manuscript.

Place	Date	Hour	Summary of Events and Information	Remarks and references to Appendices
GOUY-EN-ARTOIS	1-3-18		At 8-22 a.m. orders were received from Brigade that the Battalion would march out from the junction of Road North East of MONCHIET at 9-45 a.m. All stores were dumped. The vehicles were placed in the transport also the Battalion left GOUY-EN-ARTOIS at 9-15 a.m. On arrival at MONCHIET orders were received from the Brigade the following route march:- BEAUMETZ - SIMENCOURT - WANQUETIN - HAUTEVILLE - FOSSEUX and GOUY. The Battalion returned to billets at 2-30 p.m. A "ST DAVIDS DAY" concert was given by the Battalion in the Recreation attached to the Ecole Post Station. Special meals were provided for the men. The Regimental Band played during the evening. Arrivals 4 OR's from leave. Departures 7 OR's on leave to U.K. 2 " " " " to Italy unit	
do.	2-3-18		The Battalion was inspected at 8-30 a.m. and at 9-30 a.m. marched out for a Route March. The route was as follows:- FOSSEUX - BARLY - BAVINCOURT - COUY-EN-ARTOIS - arriving back in billets at 12-30 pm. Some fell during the morning and afternoon - the remainder of morning & physical exercises &c had been arranged. The Battalion was paid during the afternoon. Arrivals 6 OR's from leave. Departures 7 OR's on leave to U.K.	
do.	3-3-18		The Brigade route marched to BLAIRVILLE AREA. Orders were received that the Battalion would join the first Brigade N. E. of MONCHIET at 11-19 a.m. We moved out of GOUY at 10-30 a.m. and in view of the boggy state of the roads, the march was very difficult. BLAIRVILLE at 1-30 p.m. Battalion arrived at No. 2 Camp BLAIRVILLE at 1-30 p.m. Inspection and kit parade was held in the afternoon. Arrivals 3 OR's from leave. 2 Lt. J. Bukahal rejoined from hosp. Departures 7 OR's on leave to U.K.	
No. 2 Camp BLAIRVILLE	4-3-18		A test was held in Musketry for the 1st September. Every man in the Battalion altogether was tried. Each Company was allotted a time. "A" Coy 70 minutes "B" Coy 70 minutes "C" Coy 70 minutes, "D" Coy 70 minutes. The day was extremely cold and very uncomfortable and many men were suffering from nasal complaints and sore throats. In no longer distance, Zero view field is fixed. It was found that view was aimed for 70 minutes.	

Army Form C. 2118.

WAR DIARY
or
INTELLIGENCE SUMMARY.
(Erase heading not required.)

Instructions regarding War Diaries and Intelligence Summaries are contained in F. S. Regs., Part II. and the Staff Manual respectively. Title pages will be prepared in manuscript.

Place	Date	Hour	Summary of Events and Information	Remarks and references to Appendices
No 2 Camp BLAIRVILLE Camp	4-3-18		"D" Coy were on the range. The Rifles of the Battalion were inspected by the Divisional Off. The C.O. and 3 full Coy Commanders went to reconnoitre the ground over starting from Hequile N.O.R. at 1-9 pm. Before attempt to W.K. has been cut down by one half from the 5-3-18. Arrivals: 7 O.R.s returned from leave 3 " " from Hosp (sick) 2 n.c.o's & W Davies ret from line. 7 O.R.s have to list. 1 " to hosp sick.	
do.	5-3-18		Training was carried on under Company arrangements. "A" Coy used the Rifle Range 8-30 am to 12-30 pm and 1-30 pm to 3-0 pm. The troops being moved completing took place on the BLAIRVILLE hills at 4-0 pm. The band of the 13th Batt Lurry Reg. played from 5-30 pm. Arrivals. 3 O.R.s from leave	Departures. 2 O.R.s to Hospital
do.	6-3-18		The Battalion paraded at 9-0 am under Major Knight and marched to Tara's L.T. for a Brigade scheme of attack on the HENDECOURT - DUBLIN Rd Ridge. The 13th Lurry Reg carried out two companies as "MOPPERS UP" and two Companies were held in Reserve. The Battalion returned to Camp at 1-30 pm. In the afternoon, "B" & "C" Coys had Lectures Zeno Fall on the range. At 4-30 pm a Lecture was given on the BLAIRVILLE THEATRE by Lu Serge Bench on "Esperanto" Departures. Arrivals: Major W. S. Brown joined and took over command 1 O.R. from leave 1 " " furlough.	1 O.R. to Course 5 " to Hosp sick. Capt ... Russell wounded ... from leave ... form.

Army Form C. 2118.

WAR DIARY
or
INTELLIGENCE SUMMARY.

(Erase heading not required.)

Instructions regarding War Diaries and Intelligence Summaries are contained in F. S. Regs., Part II. and the Staff Manual respectively. Title pages will be prepared in manuscript.

Place	Date	Hour	Summary of Events and Information	Remarks and references to Appendices
No 2 Camp Busigny	7-3-18		The Battalion paraded at 9-15 a.m. under Major W. S. Brown and marched off at 9-30 a.m. to the assembly point for a Brigade scheme of attack. The scheme was a repetition of the scheme carried out on the previous day. ZERO hour was at 11-0 a.m. and the final advance was taken at 12-15 p.m. The Divisional Commander was present at the scheme. Each Battalion formed up after the attack and marched back to camp. During the day a "Board of Enquiry" was held in the Recreation Room of its Battalion & later a Co operation of Infantry and Tanks demonstration was held. Efforts on the theatre. B.O.O. V/125.	
			Arrivals	
			1 O.R. from Base.	
			1 " from Hospital	
do	8-3-18		The 119th Infantry Brigade was inspected by the Corps Commander. The Battalion paraded at 9-30 a.m. and marched on to Vicoigne [?] where the parade arrived at 10-0 a.m. Inspection was down the ranks. His & Co. Commanders & Company Ground Liaison Section in the rest the 229 & Lewis Gunners R.F. and the 119 T.M. Battery in the rear. Five paces between ranks. The Bands of the 13th East Surreys and 18th Welch were massed, 20 paces in rear of the centre of the Bns. All moved to Company formation. Field the inspection from 2 p.m. to 3-30 p.m. A cross country run competition arranged platoons of 30 O.R. were held. It came 2nd with the 2nd lasting time 15 min. Winning Platoon No 7. B. Co. Brown. The Morale Competition.	
			Arrivals	
			1 O.R. from Base.	
				D.W. Aupurs
				3 O.R.'s to Base & ops
				1 " to Hospital

WAR DIARY or INTELLIGENCE SUMMARY.

Army Form C. 2118.

(Erase heading not required.)

Place	Date	Hour	Summary of Events and Information	Remarks and references to Appendices
No 2 Camp HAIREVILLE	9-3-18		In the morning from 8.30 am to 12.30 "A" "B" and "D" Coys carried out Close Order Drill and a Battalion attack on a small system of trenches. "C" Coy had firing practice on the range and the Lewis Gun Teams had firing practice with Lewis Guns. Four Officers and all ranks but N.C.O's attended a demonstration of anti-aircraft work with Lewis Guns at the Regimental M.G. Instructor. Brigade wiring competitions were held on the Field at 5 p.m. Awards 8 O.R's Funderes [?]	Lectures N.C.O's / 2 Lectures in the morning 1 O.R. to Hospital 1 nco. left 3 Battalion Games Hours Lectures Infantry 3 O.R's on cmd to unit
do	10-3-18		Church Parade was held at 11.15 am on the Battalion Parade Ground. Lieut Rowe was in attendance. The Commanding Officer Inspected and Company Commanders the Commanders and the Transport of all the D Coys from The Regt Officers Club at Bowl at 5pm. Lecture 7 O.R's from Army Reinforce 3 " from Corps Hospital	3 O.R's on cmd to unit
do	11-3-18		Training was carried on under Battalion arrangements from 8.30 to 11.30. 12 to 4 pm and 4.30 to 4.30 pm. "D" Coy had firing practice on the range and the Lewis Gun Teams also had firing practice with Lewis Guns. A demonstration was given to all officers on the Battalion Training Ground of the formations to be adopted by Infantry when confronting with Tanks. All Companies looked during the day at HAIREVILLE Bath. Arrivals 3 O.R's from Camp 1 " from Hospital	24 Reinfs 3 O.R's sent to unit 2 " to Hospital

Instructions regarding War Diaries and Intelligence Summaries are contained in F. S. Regs., Part II. and the Staff Manual respectively. Title pages will be prepared in manuscript.

WAR DIARY
or
INTELLIGENCE SUMMARY.
(Erase heading not required.)

Army Form C. 2118.

Place	Date	Hour	Summary of Events and Information	Remarks and references to Appendices
No. 2 Camp BLAIREVILLE	12-3-18		The programme of training was carried on during the morning. An advance party of 1 Officer and 9 O.R. started at 2-0 p.m. by motor lorry for NORTHUMBERLAND LINES. MERCATEL to take over the camp from the [illegible]. A portion of the camp was allotted to a Company of the Machine Gun Battalion. The Battalion moved out at 6-30 p.m. The [illegible] marched out of BLAIREVILLE CAMP at [illegible] p.m. and arrived at NORTHUMBERLAND LINES at 7-15 p.m. Details were left at HENDECOURT Camp under Major Stratton. An attack by the enemy on the VI Corps front was expected this morning the 13th inst.	
			Arrivals: 5 O.R. returned from leave. 7 [illegible] specials from I.B.D. 2/Lt. G.H. Jones returned from leave.	
			Departures: Major [illegible] proceeded to England on [illegible] leave of absence. 3 O.R. on leave to U.K. 1 " to hospital sick.	
NORTHUMBERLAND LINES. MERCATEL	13-3-18		Training was carried on from 9-0 a.m. to 4-30 p.m. "D" Coy had musketry practice on the range. All other companies had Close Order Drill, [illegible] fighting and [illegible] training. The Corps front has been quiet all day. 2nd Lt. [illegible] Turnbull returned from leave & [illegible] O.R. on leave to U.K. and 4 O.R. returned from leave.	
do	14-3-18		The training was carried on as yesterday. A Coy were on the range during the morning. The situation on the Corps front has been quiet. A little rain fell early this morning. The wind still remains cold.	
			Arrivals: 7 O.R. returned from leave	
			Departures: 3 O.R. on leave to U.K.	
do	15-3-18		At 7-5 a.m. the message "HUN PREPARE" was received from Brigade. The Battalion at once packed up and fell in ready to move out. This was completed inside 40 minutes. The order then came to stand down and training was proceeded with on the usual lines.	
			Arrivals: 1 O.R. returned from leave	
			Departures: 3 O.R. on leave to U.K. 2nd Lieut. H. Duff to hospital sick from course. 2 O.R. to hospital sick. 2nd Lieut. Davis granted leave to U.K.	

(A7092). Wt. W12839/M1293. 750,000. 1/17. D. D. & L., Ltd. Forms/C.2118/14.

WAR DIARY
or
INTELLIGENCE SUMMARY.
(Erase heading not required.)

Army Form C. 2118.

Instructions regarding War Diaries and Intelligence Summaries are contained in F.S. Regs., Part II. and the Staff Manual respectively. Title pages will be prepared in manuscript.

Place	Date	Hour	Summary of Events and Information	Remarks and references to Appendices
NORTHERN GARLAND LINES MERCATEL	16-3-18		The Battalion on usual training. The Inter Bn. & int Company Rifle meet of the mulches were played.	
			Arrivals	
			3 O.R. from base to unit.	
		11 O.R. returned from leave.	Departures	
				2 O.R. to hospital
Do	17-3-18		Church Parade during the morning. During the afternoon the enemy Bn working parties 163 O.R. went out at 5.30 p.m. to make dugouts for Brigade staff. They did not return from the bombing. They received heavy shell fire when going out &p.m. 18-3-18.	
			A lecture was given to the officers by Lt. W.J. Stephe (R.A.M.C.) who served the Battalion in England in 1916. He joined the Battalion in 1916.	
			Arrivals	Departures
			6 O.R. from Base	3 O.R. Base to unit
			19 " " " 1 A.D.	1 " to hospital
Do	18-3-18		During the late afternoon & evening parties put up wire where wire cut & knocked out. 10-0 p.m. The evening was comparatively quiet after the systematic shell bombardment on [?] Artillery P.H. 300 along was given permission to remain in Arras until midnight till 6-30 p.m.	
			Arrivals	Departures
			2nd Lt J.C. Oakley 1 O.R.	2nd Lt R.C. Higgins to [?]
			8 O.R. returned from Base	3 W.R to hospital.
			1 " " " hospital	
Do	19-3-18		Training was carried on during the morning. Parties in the attack. Rain & no firing during the afternoon. Work on Brigade dugouts continued. Working parties of 200 along were found during the Bayou Cete Boil - see appendix. at 5.0 p.m.	
			Arrivals	Departures
			3 O.R. returned from leave	3 O.R to hospital
			Lieut S.J. Ground joined from N.A.R.	1 O.R. to Musketry School
			1 O.R. to attachment to [?]	

WAR DIARY
or
INTELLIGENCE SUMMARY.
(Erase heading not required.)

Place	Date	Hour	Summary of Events and Information	Remarks and references to Appendices
NORTHUMBERLAND LINES (MERCATEL)	21-3-18		Jan. 1. Demonstration attended by Brigadier & Staff and Coys. Commanders also other officers and observers. Arrivals 1 OR Joined Bn.	
			2 OR to hospital	
do	21-3-18	5-0 a.m.	At 5-0 a.m. the Battalion received orders to "stand to" ready. At 5-30 a.m. the Battalion received orders to move to HAMELINCOURT & took up their main defensive position.	
		7-45 a.m.	At 6-30 a.m. the Battalion moved off to a position in BOISLEUX front line facing (?) St. MARC.	
		5-30 a.m.	Orders were then received to move to the SENSEE SWITCH on the RIGHT BANK of the river of the following position & holding the switch from the RAILWAY SYSTEM headquarters at JUDAS FARM. "B" Coy's HQ. with the RAILWAY on JUDAS FARM. "C" Coy on a position near RAILWAY on the same road at T.11.b. (T.11.c.) & junction with the DEMI LINE. "D" Coy TODAS FARM. & Battn. HQ. at the mill at BOYELLES and the Battn. HQ were moved to the same place at T7.10.c holding CROISILLES heavily. One BATTERY were my active and 7.10.a the enemy shelled CROISILLES heavily.	
		12-15 p.m.	No attempt made by the enemy to advance.	
		1-05 p.m.	The enemy moved his front CROISILLES & he ordered the 105 behind the T.6.1. as we thought it necessary to keep out a defensive flank to protect our left. One Platoon of DRAY Coy then got in touch with the RAILWAY EMBANKMENT.	
		2 p.m.	We in touch right and centre with guides support from the FIRST STAGE of advance.	
		2 p.m.	We in touch right & left on touch at 7.22 in hollow about SENSEE SWITCH	
			At 7.16.6 on batn right STEEPER CAN of BURY DAY in holding a short front on account of T.16.8	
		2-30 a.m.	Orders were then received from Brigade HQ to make clear the houses in STEEPER BANK. Patrols were then sent found again. The village is still clear of the enemy.	

WAR DIARY
or
INTELLIGENCE SUMMARY.
(Erase heading not required.)

Place	Date	Hour	Summary of Events and Information	Remarks and references to Appendices
In the Field	22.3.18	2a.m.	The Batt. has fallen back to a position to defend the village to the N.W.	
		3.45 a.m.	The enemy advanced over the high ground in W14. A & C coming in the direction of ST LEGER. These were caught by our Artillery and badly broken up.	
		4.45 a.m.	It was reported that the 102nd Bde. and M.G.ppers[?] Bn. Line and that the East Yorks had returned to their line near ST LEGER. The enemy still holding ST LEGER.	
		5.2 p.m.	Our patrol returning from ST LEGER report that a large body of the enemy had fallen into ST LEGER. Northumberland Fusiliers Lane fallen back on to our Line.	
		5.20 p.m.	ST LEGER again clear of the enemy who are in HINDENBURG in large numbers.	
	about 6.0 p.m.	Enemy advanced from HILL SWITCH (T.27.d) over the high ground in T.27.c. Our Reserve Company was at once ordered to man the Reserve Line, to hold a good front from T.27.a.4.3 to K.6.9.7.27 & 2.8. F.O.O. by pre-arranged sig. on the road received two Trench Mortars & one new bomb surrounded and was brought in. The Zouave section of our machine guns took up new position to the S. & W. They shortly afterwards retired under orders from the Batt. on left and later the R. M. L. I. Bde. opened some long .303 at K.4.10 on the enemy who came up in Hundreds to hold signal the church TRESCAULT FARM. The relieved Bn. Coy Reserve by 3 units of... ... was used at Cross Roads T.23. b. Central. 2 Lewis Guns & the machine gun was placed in the Road near KOH TAM ... near ST LEGER and advised of all positions. The machine of K.H. 11 opened ... and our artillery fire up on Cross Road and The guns had opened. But ... was held but the SENSEE SWITCH, SENSEE SWITCH, M.G. to await the SENSEE SWITCH, Railway around TRESCAULT ... and demolished at night. 20 Pigeons were dropped. Orders had been received to man... B.F.A.M. support and if necessary recapture the ARMY LINE which had been taken over by the British Bde. & Battalion moved off at 6.30 a.m. and concentrated on by 8.30 a.m. The Brigade and East Yorks were ordered to recapture the left bank of the line and the Welch were to... ... The enemy attacked TRAIN B.F.A. at the same time but the Brigade for Army Field Ambulance on the	
CROSS ROADS NORTH OF JUDAS FARM	23.3.18	5.0 a.m. 10.0 a.m.		

WAR DIARY
or
INTELLIGENCE SUMMARY.
(Erase heading not required.)

Instructions regarding War Diaries and Intelligence Summaries are contained in F.S. Regs., Part II. and the Staff Manual respectively. Title pages will be prepared in manuscript.

Place	Date	Hour	Summary of Events and Information	Remarks and references to Appendices
CROSS ROADS NORTH OF TILGES FARM.	23-3-18	11-15 AM	The 13th Fort Garage on 11.44 4:30 A and B11.c — Suffers at R19 central — Rest Brigade Engaged at NURLU Junction. B33.b.	
		12-15 PM	A G.O.M. sent out to reconnoitre 2nd Battalion who had fallen Back by Guards amount. The Group assembled to like MARY COPPE 2nd Battalion tired from the North of B.M.C.B.2 at MARY COPSE and R.H. Bullogues with machine gun fire to Best of B.M.C.B.2. Gave orders not refuse and fight to Last Round. B.M. 1.2.L. of B11.c.4.8 sent out. 2nd hostilities about the enemy tried to out flank B.M. and had Garage forced to stop back on edge of MURCH VILLAGE. Enemy getting assisted men Enemy artillery quite.	
		1-15 PM	Advised on observing that with A.H.Q. Brig. new Base applied the Brigade in 197.7. B.M. at Norman battalion to B.15.C.O.2. W.V. who moved to B.12.R.5.5. Waiting for help. W.M.D. at Nurman battalion to C.R.B.12.A. All troops dug in Lowe Redoubts Did not send headquarter to the arrivals and only when Kv got handed to Bitty. MARY COPSE had to be defended to the Last Many to be act.	
		2 PM	Held out all day. Enemy attempt Kurd to on Ridge was Burposet of goal Engage to refund and Nort. Kurd of the Kurd.	
		10-20 PM	The S. Lenand. From 2nd battalion — ment there to be largest Engagement of the Kurd of the Kurd on a reduced front ands the Kurd to Leve enough this 2nd of reduced front to NURLY vid. B12.A.B.9. 2nd at T10. Lot recognise Rest information plans. 5.23 behind R21.a.9. would live rest of the DILBUT to army to reserve lean. Though at by line told the Tr tives that work to reinforced R17 M.G. My left below it by line the line hear the Sort of Nurman by Railway cutting MURCH COPSE and sword between then and that Canadian Valley for hopped the Ravine between both and the trenches to Ervilleum Living the Kent as a subject line with R.H.Q. QUARRY who had rest reg.q. held who had rest reg.q.	
	25	6 AM		

WAR DIARY or INTELLIGENCE SUMMARY

Army Form C. 2118.

Place	Date	Hour	Summary of Events and Information	Remarks and references to Appendices
	25-3-18		Battalion [illegible] to form a line through B.H.Q. and 2/ Suffolks [illegible] to establish [illegible] which was employed in covering ENGINEERS [illegible] to [illegible] and support this against attack from EAU CLAIR. At dusk received orders to withdraw via HAMEL MONT – COURCELLES – LEBOEUF – AYETTE – BUCQUOY – arrived at MONCHY at 1.30 a.m. Men had [illegible] march.	
	26-3-18		Received orders to form Reserve to Sgt. General ADINFER WOOD — 2/4th Division were to hold line detailed as Support Batln. and Bn. H.Q. line East of ADINFER.	
	27-3-18		Received orders to move back to SOMBRIN. [illegible] path to MONCHY — gave much attack and arrived at 3 a.m. the next day — BOY to SOMBRIN arriving about 6 a.m. — men had a meal and slept. [illegible] village in morning, not encouraging.	
SOMBRIN	28/3/18		Resting all day — Batt. orders issued [illegible] SOMBRIN. [illegible] during the situation — [illegible] killed, 11 [illegible], 79 missing, 119 wounded. Officers: Capt. J. S. McGarry killed in action. Capt. E. A. W. Brown missing. 2/Lt. C. H. Brown — " 2/Lt. J. J. Dunn — " " L. G. Prichard — " " J. G. Pritchard — " " J. G. Parker — " " T. R. Parker. Lt. E. J. Tindale wounded [illegible].	
	29-3-18		Batt. orders received to proceed to MONCHY – BRETON then by foot march – route AVESNES-LE-COMTE – TINCQUES. En route destination changed from FREVILLERS to DIEVAL. Arrived in billets at DIEVAL at 4.30 p.m. Battn. of [illegible] and [illegible].	
DIEVAL	30-3-18		Kit inspection and [illegible] the Battalion. [illegible] organization of Platoons and Companies. 2 O.R. to hospital sick. [illegible]	

Army Form C. 2118.

WAR DIARY
or
INTELLIGENCE SUMMARY.
(Erase heading not required.)

Instructions regarding War Diaries and Intelligence Summaries are contained in F. S. Regs., Part II. and the Staff Manual respectively. Title pages will be prepared in manuscript.

Place	Date	Hour	Summary of Events and Information	Remarks and references to Appendices
DIEVAL	31-3-18		Echelon "B" – Bd C at 11-0 a.m. in field near Rly 10" K.8" bivouced and erected 4 tents. Dinner at 11-0 a.m. Remainder of day spent resting. Arrivals Nil.	

40th Division.
119th Infantry Brigade.

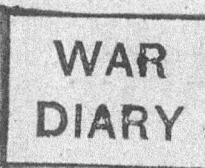

18th BATTALION

THE WELCH REGIMENT

APRIL 1918

Attached :- Report on Operations 9th-14th April

Army Form C. 2118.

WAR DIARY
or
INTELLIGENCE SUMMARY.
(Erase heading not required.)

18 M.G.Bn. 119/4 W.C.2

War Diary.
April 1918.

Army Form C. 2118.

WAR DIARY
or
INTELLIGENCE SUMMARY.

(Erase heading not required.)

Place	Date	Hour	Summary of Events and Information	Remarks and references to Appendices
DIEVAL	1-4-19		Battalion ordered to proceed by route march to BARLIN. Entrain on Railway at FOSSE LA-DITA – BARLIN on route to DOULIEU AREA. Having [?] four [?] – 10 Coys at 7.45 am and - HOUDAIN – MAISNIL – RUITZ BRUAY. Battalion entrained about 11-30 a.m and arrived at RIBECQ near NEUF BERQUIN at [?] and marched to [?] at RUE MENTON - Battalion HQrs in Farm C369, Transport Bypassed and ordered to proceed from DIEVAL by route ROME – BRUAY – MARLES – LES MINES – LIBECOURT – Stationing at C [?] – DIVISION 11-0 am. Battalion stayed night [?] at [?]. Arrival.	
ROBECOURT	2/4/18		Battalion ordered to proceed by hycle route to NEUF BERQUIN prep to [?] SAILLY-SUR-LA-LYS at 11-5 a.m. Rode NEUF BERQUIN – ESTAIRES. Battalion arrived in billets at [?] along with rest Front PONTLEVIS G 2 c d (map Croix-du-Bac) Eastern [?] [?] Headquarters at Brewery B 26 a 9.1 Transport arrived at [?] Farm at H-30 k.m at TROU BAYARD B 20 a (Sheet) [?] Service	
ESTAIRES	3/4/18		Battalion ordered to move to ESTAIRES and took over cars in Hulls marching out of billets at 11-0 am. [?]	
"	4/4/18		Conference Battalion at SAILLY with arrived our am. Training	
"	5/4/18		[?] Training. C.O. Officer recommended Defensive Scale with French Batts.	

Army Form C. 2118.

WAR DIARY
or
INTELLIGENCE SUMMARY.
(Erase heading not required.)

Instructions regarding War Diaries and Intelligence Summaries are contained in F. S. Regs., Part II. and the Staff Manual respectively. Title pages will be prepared in manuscript.

Place	Date 1918	Hour	Summary of Events and Information	Remarks and references to Appendices
ESTAIRES & FLEURBAIX SECTOR	April 6		Preparing to go into the line. Bussed in rear of camp at 5 p.m. My platoon at 10.45 pm interval and relieved the 19th Bn. R.I. in the Right Sub Sector FLEURBAIX. B. Co. H.S. at 11.2 a.m. 7.4.18. Relief completed without incident.	
"	7	My 9.27 pm	Night quiet. Desperal met with no enemy + lines of enemy	
"	8		Busy firing on improvement of the line. Patrols on right hand side contacted enemy.	
"	9		As above. A very quiet day. At 10.45 pm 9/1 Hill and 9/Ir.Fus. Bn. manned & Patrol met Enemy lines reconnoitering Machine trench and NEPTUNE TRENCH returning at 2.30 pm. and reported all quiet.	
A		At 4.20 am	Enemy barrage on front line and extended as far as… "Bee" fought a rearguard action until 19th April. See Narrative attached. marked A	A
B	13 14	8 am	Bn marched from STAPLE to TILQUES via ST OMER arriving there about 3.30 pm. Went into Billets A.	
	15	2-6 pm	Bn marched to MOULLE and went into billets there arriving 6 pm	

Army Form C. 2118.

WAR DIARY
or
INTELLIGENCE SUMMARY.

(Erase heading not required.)

Instructions regarding War Diaries and Intelligence Summaries are contained in F.S. Regs., Part II. and the Staff Manual respectively. Title pages will be prepared in manuscript.

Place	Date 1918 APRIL	Hour	Summary of Events and Information	Remarks and references to Appendices
WIZERNES	16	—	Batt" buried at training at CORNETTE (? ground) at 4.30 p.m. returned WS.	
"	17	"	10th training ground and returned at 4.30 p.m. WS. Batt" training as above from 8.0 am – 3.30 p.m. Div. Engr. on the range WS.	
"	18	"	Very hot day. Carried on training in Billets. WS	
"	19	"	Two companies firing on range, remainder on training area. Also Div. Drill Ammunition Inspected. WS	
"	20	"	Kit Inspection. Hair Cutting and Inspection by G.O.C. men on full marching order. Afternoon — football games. WS	
"	21	—	Church parade at 9.30 am. The Assistant Chaplain General addressed the men. At 2.0 p.m. Bn. billets received orders and commenced to ZUDAUSQUES. Marching completed at 4.50 p.m. WS	
ZUDAUSQUES	22		Batt" training B & C Coys firing on range all morning. WS	

Army Form C. 2118.

WAR DIARY
or
INTELLIGENCE SUMMARY.
(Erase heading not required.)

Instructions regarding War Diaries and Intelligence Summaries are contained in F.S. Regs., Part II. and the Staff Manual respectively. Title pages will be prepared in manuscript.

Place	Date	Hour	Summary of Events and Information	Remarks and references to Appendices
ZUDAUSQUES	23/4/18		Bath Parade. All day. 1 + B Coys. Firing on range. Kit inspn. Rifle Inspection by Armourer Sergeant.	
ZUDAUSQUES	24/4/18		Battn training.	
ZUDAUSQUES	25/4/18		Battn training.	
ZUDAUSQUES	26/4/18		Battn training. A reconnaissance with Battn Lewis gun letter No R18(A) dated 24/4/18 (K+N R18(A)) detach relating to provision of Establishment for Training Musketry nominal roll has been commenced.	
ZUDAUSQUES	27/4/18		Mining School came temporarily into ... two reports signed present at Depot of VIII Corps. The Battn forming part of Corps Res. No 2 moving to be in move to STAPLE area ... Battn training suspended.	
ZUDAUSQUES	28/4/18		Church Parade 11.30 A.M. Battn being held in attendance. R.C. troops in usual ... transferred in Camp 60 yards orders re move ...	
ZUDAUSQUES	29/4/18		Batt. training resumed. A + B Coys march at ACQUIN. During drill to proceed to ST MOMELIN via the North Travel. CO moved for recce with ...	
MOMELIN (BOIS DU HAM)	30/4/18		CO + 2 Coys proceeded to reconnoitre proposed defense line E. of POPERINGHE. The Battn moved at 7 A.M. and passed initial starting point STRINGHEM 8.56 A.M. The Act. Adjutant detailed to command No 2 Advance Brigade on the journey. Battn started Billets at BOIS DU HAM ... good and arrived 12.30 P.M. Warning orders to move on 1st May to REMIELD then received at 9 P.M.	

"A"

8th Batt" The Queen's Regt.
Narrative of Events 9th April to 14th Apr. 1918.

The Batt" was on the night 8/9 April 1918 holding the line in the Right sub section of the FLEURBAIX SECTOR, having the Portuguese Corps on the Right and the 13th East Surreys on the Left.

At 10.00 pm on the 8th 2/Lt. Ho-ttitt and Lt. A Bullett with 10 O.R. made a reconnaissance into the Enemy lines working down NECKLACE and HEBREW TRENCHES they found the trenches and No mans land waterlogged. The patrol returned about 2.0 am having seen no signs of the Enemy.

At 4.15 am our Artillery put down a heavy Barrage on the enemy front line till 4.50 am and again from 5.10 to 5.30 am

At 4.25 am the enemy Barraged our front line & also shelled heavily the support line and all tracks.

At 5.55 am a message was received from O.C. Right Bank Coy that the Enemy was coming over on the Portuguese front in large numbers & that the barrage had moved to our support line. EXETER

2.

Avenue had been manned by the Reserve
Company on the outbreak of the shelling.
           At 4.30am the enemy also put
over gas shells mixed with his H.E.
           At 6.0am the enemy broke through
between our ~~Reserve~~ Left Post and the First
Batt'n on our left in large
numbers. Spread along the front line
towards our Right and advanced on our
Support line.
           The posts in the front line were
apparently cut off as the garrison did
not fall back on to the support line.
           The Support line Garrison put up
a good defence. 40 dead Germans being
counted in front of No 12 L.G. Post, and
30 in front of a post on the right.
           I sent up two Platoons of my
Support Coy to reinforce the support
line at 7.0am on receipt of message that
the enemy was on the line.
           O.C. Right Coy reported at 8.0am
that intense fire was being put on the
support line, & at 8.20am that the
Barrage had lifted and that he was
surrounded by the enemy in large
numbers but was holding on to the

3

kant. There are no survivors of this Coy.

By 9 am what left Batt Coy remnants had been forced back down Impertinence AVENUE on to the road and reported the enemy in large numbers advancing down Impertinence and VC Avenues. At the same time the enemy put down intense fire on B.H.Q. destroying the mess and Headquarters Coy. Billets.

At 9.40 am. the Russian force had advanced with hine VC Avenue and Impertinence Avenue. I detailed my two Reserve L.G. to hold the road here. Both points & teams were wiped out within 10 minutes by shell fire.

At 10:00 am the enemy being within 100 yards of B.H.Q I decided to evacuate as well. The remnants of the H.Q and fought a rear guard action in the direction of WINTERS NIGHT POST accounting for many of the enemy who were within point blank range and at the same time sustaining many casualties including my Adjutant Intelligence Officer and L.G. Officer.

At 10.45 am I arrived at

4

Wuslus Kright Post which was
garrisoned by a detachment of 21 Middlesex
 I drew 4 boxes of SAA from their
B.H.Q. but on endeavouring to return to
the post found it was surrounded by
the enemy who were advancing on
Reserve B.H.Q.   The Garrison at the
Post including the 21 Middlesex and 18th
heads were practically wiped out
with shell fire and M.G. fire and only
a very few were able to fall back.

My reserve Coy which manned
GASPAR AVENUE by posts as far
as CHARRED POST put up a strong
resistance. The O.C. Coy being dangerously
wounded. The enemy took them in
front, flank, & rear and the whole Coy
is now missing.

Out of the Troops holding the
line on the night 5/6 April only
Two officers myself & Squadron officer
and 20 O.R survived.

And I had now no troops left to
command. I made my way to B.H.C.
STAAPE hoping to find some of my
men on the road to reorganise but
found none. Secured a L.G. with two men
whom I placed to hold the pontoon

bridge here. The Gun's Bee of the howier
were knocked out with a shell.
I then reported to Brigade at CROIX
DU BAC and went on to LE PT MORTIER

10th April

At 4.20 am. I was given the 119 Inf Brigade
Composite Battn and instructed to take up
a position in the STEEN WERCK SWITCH
which I did with 2 Midd on Right
Surreys and ? 12 Gurs. Details of other
Brigade the line running from
G.10.b. central to LE KORLEZ in
front of LES MORTIER with BHQ at
LE PT MORTIER.
Owing to the with Flank falling
back I had to conform & the right
rested at 4 pm on G.3.d.2.0. and
the left Flank on A.28.a.2.6. This
Position was held all day. The Enemy
shelled very heavily at intervals.
The 100 I.B. Composite Battn were in
touch on the left.
Patrols were sent out during the
day to La BOUDRELLE SAILLY
and CROIX DU BAC setting in
touch with troops in front

6

At 3-15pm the enemy were observed at
A29.a.40-90. At 3.50pm the
enemy broke through our line at
pt BANKSTEAD & the line was forced
back to 28.a. At 6.10pm Div
informed that Division on the left
had fallen back. At 6.45pm I took
my line back to A28.d-30.5 but
at 7.20pm had again to conform with
the line on left and withdrew to
A28.c.
        This final position was held all
night which was quiet except for
M.G. fire.

April 11"
        At 3.25AM 2. S.W.B. & K.O.S.B. reported
and took up a position in our rear.
At 7.10 am the enemy shelled the front
line heavily. BHQ was at A26.d-8.5
8.0 am O.C. 21" Middlesex reported that
the enemy were gaining superiority
of fire on our right flank and
detached 2 M.G" to cover his flank
        The enemy who were in G10.c+d
kept up heavy fire. About 11.0 am
the enemy put down an intense
barrage including 5" on H.Q

line & advanced under M.G. Fire. Both
of our flanks gave way, and our
line had to give way taking up a
position through G.2.c.5.7. and
A.27.d.2.8. About 11.0.am. The
Enemy barraged this line with very
heavy stuff and also demolished
B.H.Q. farm. The Enemy broke
through on both flanks & the line
again fell back on to the STEENBEEK
ROAD where the 119 & 120 Brigades
were reorganised on a line in
front of LE PELERIER APPROX.
A.20.a.5.0. to A.26.c.0.7. Their
line was organised in depth + a
forward line on the railway.

The Enemy shelled continuously
and also fired flanking M.G. Fire

This line was held all night
About 7.0pm the enemy appeared
to try a sortie from about A.21
central but was suppressed by our
M.G. Fire. From 9.0pm
onwards he was quiet.

Apl 12 At 8.25 am the 92nd Brigade
completed the taking over of this

line covering our positions and I withdrew the 119th & 120th Composite Batts. to STRAZEELE arriving there about 11.30 pm. The relief was completed without incident.

After the men had a meal instructions were received to dig & man a line for the defence of STRAZEELE on the E & S side of the village. This was cancelled later and the 119 I.B. Composite Batt: was given the E side.

This line was set out and men were in position & digging by 4.0 pm.
The line ran (Haydrook map) due E through A in STRAZEELE to road junction S of 6 in 620 then South to get in touch with 121 Brigade — 21 Middx on Right, 1st E. Surreys in Centre & 18 Welsh on left.

Many patrols were sent out all night both to front and flanks and information sent to Brigade. The line was heavily shelled till dusk but the night was quiet.

Apl 13 During the early morning considerable shelling took place. A division of the Anzac Corps having taken up a position in front of us (4th Australian Div'n) during the night. Instructions were received to withdraw the troops to PRADELLES and this was completed by 12·30 p.m. The Combined Troops of the Brigade then marched to LE BREARDE - Had a meal and marched to STAPLE, and lay there the night

Apl. 14.
Marching at 8.0 am to TILQUES where they were Billetted

Apl. 15
And moving again to MOULLE the next day to Billets -

W S Brown
Lt Col
Commandg. 18th Welsh

16/4/18

CONFIDENTIAL.

18th (S.) Bn THE WELSH REGIMENT.

WAR DIARY

Volume No.

MAY 1918

Army Form C. 2118.

WAR DIARY
or
INTELLIGENCE SUMMARY.

(Erase heading not required.)

War Diary

of

14th D.A.C.

Place	Date	Hour	Summary of Events and Information	Remarks and references to Appendices

Instructions regarding War Diaries and Intelligence Summaries are contained in F. S. Regs., Part II. and the Staff Manual respectively. Title pages will be prepared in manuscript.

Army Form C. 2118.

WAR DIARY
or
INTELLIGENCE SUMMARY.
(Erase heading not required.)

Instructions regarding War Diaries and Intelligence Summaries are contained in F.S. Regs., Part II. and the Staff Manual respectively. Title pages will be prepared in manuscript.

Place	Date	Hour	Summary of Events and Information	Remarks and references to Appendices
ST MOMELIN [BOIS-DU-HAM]	1.5.18		The Battalion proceeded by march route to TWELD Area. Tents were received at TERDEGHEM.	G/N
TERDEGHEM	2.5.18		The Commanding Officer & Company Commanders reconnoitred the WATOU Area. The Battalion paraded for the purpose of cleaning equipment & clothing. At 5.30pm orders were received for the Battalion to move to ST MOMELIN [BOIS-DU-HAM] Area. The Battalion marched from HUTS at 7.30pm & proceeded by march route.	G/N
BOIS-DU-HAM	3.5.18		The Battalion held an inspection of feet & also clothing. The remainder of the day was spent in resting the men.	G/N
BOIS-DU-HAM	4.5.18		The Battalion held a recreation & parade under the supervision of the Quartermaster. A Battalion Dinner was given in the evening.	G/N
BOIS-DU-HAM	5.5.18		The Battalion numbering 7 Officers & 787 ORs less the training establishment were despatched to the Base. This party commanded from HUTS at 2.30pm & entrained at ST OMER at 5pm for CALAIS. The Senior Officer [Lt HAY M.C.] was in command.	G/N
BOIS-DU-HAM	6.5.18		The personnel of the training establishment paraded for Kit inspection. The Commanding Officer held a conference of all officers.	G/N

Army Form C. 2118.

WAR DIARY
or
INTELLIGENCE SUMMARY.
(Erase heading not required.)

Instructions regarding War Diaries and Intelligence Summaries are contained in F. S. Regs., Part II. and the Staff Manual respectively. Title pages will be prepared in manuscript.

Place	Date	Summary of Events and Information	Remarks and references to Appendices
BOIS-DU-HAM	7.5.18	The Battalion paraded for inspection & drill. The Orderly Officer was in charge of the parade.	O/f
BOIS-DU-HAM	8.5.18	a Boots & Clothing inspection was held by the Quartermaster after which a Physical Training & Bayonet Fighting under the Supervision of the Orderly Officer. Baths were attended at ST MOMELIN from 12.0 noon to 2.0 pm.	O/f
BOIS-DU-HAM	9.5.18	Inspection parade at 10 am by the Orderly Officer. Physical Training + Bayonet Fighting which carried out during the morning. Orders were issued to move next day to STAPLE Area.	O/f
BOIS-DU-HAM	10.5.18	The training Battalion proceeded by march to STAPLE Area. Route as follows:— ST MOMELIN – LEDERZEELE – B__ BAEMBERG – E__ L'HEY – LES SIX RUES – STAPLE. The Battalion moved off at 9 am & arrived at destination by 4.15 pm. a distance of 20 miles. Billets. MSSSW Hato were reached at Aerodrome P.25.C.7.7. 27.0.15.	O/f
STAPLE [AERODROME] P.25.C.7.7	11.5.18	Inspection Parade at 10 am under the Orderly Officer. P.T. & D.T. Route. The Commanding Officer Adjutant & Coy Commander reconnoitred the WINNEZEELE DEFENSE Line.	O/f

A7092. Wt. W1839g/M1293. 750,000. 1/17. D.D & I. Ltd. Forms/Carr B/14.

Army Form C. 2118.

WAR DIARY
or
INTELLIGENCE SUMMARY.
(Erase heading not required.)

Instructions regarding War Diaries and Intelligence Summaries are contained in F. S. Regs., Part II. and the Staff Manual respectively. Title pages will be prepared in manuscript.

Place	Date	Hour	Summary of Events and Information	Remarks and references to Appendices
STAPLE [AERODROME] P.26.c.7.7.	12.5.18		Orderly Room was held at 10 a.m. Members of the 17th Klu Balloon Section attended. In the afternoon the Battalion played the Balloon Section in Association football. The Battalion winning by 4 goals to 1.	QM
STAPLE [AERODROME] P.25.c.7.7.	13.5.18		The following training programme was carried out under Supervision of the orderly officer. Arms Drill, Communication Drill, Gas Instruction, P.T., & Bayonet fighting. Company Commanders & Specialist Officers reconnoitred the HAZEBROUCK Defence System.	QM
STAPLE [AERODROME] P.25.c.7.7.	14.5.18		Parades 10 a.m. Infantry Physical training Communication Drill Guard mounting &c. Company Commanders and Specialist Officers reconnoitred the HAZEBROUCK Defence System.	QM
STAPLE [AERODROME] P.25.c.7.7.	15.5.18		The Battalion vacated the Nissen huts at the Aerodrome and pitched tents at O.30.a.2.2.	QM
STAPLE O.30.a.2.2.	16.5.18		Company Commanders & N.C.Os reconnoitred the HAZEBROUCK Defence System.	QM

Army Form C. 2118.

WAR DIARY
or
INTELLIGENCE SUMMARY.
(Erase heading not required.)

Instructions regarding War Diaries and Intelligence Summaries are contained in F. S. Regs., Part II. and the Staff Manual respectively. Title pages will be prepared in manuscript.

Place	Date	Hour	Summary of Events and Information	Remarks and references to Appendices
STAPLE O.30.a.2.2	17.5.18		Battns were attached at ST MARIE-CAPPEL at 10.0 am. Coy Commds T.N.C.Os completed the reconnaissance of the HAZEBROUCK Defence System.	W4
STAPLE O.30.a.2.2	18.5.18		The Commanding Officer inspected the Personnel of the Training Establishment at 10. am. The men were paid at 3pm.	W4
STAPLE O.30.a.2.2	19.5.18		A combined C of E & Nonconformist Service was held at 10. am. R.Cs attended at the church at ST MARIE-CAPPEL at 11.0 am.	W4
STAPLE O.30.a.2.2	20.5.18		The following Training Programme was carried out during the morning – Physical training, Communication Drill, Guard Mounting, Gas Instruction.	W4
STAPLE O.30.a.2.2	21.5.18		The Training Establishment paraded for an hours physical training & then attended the full Company Commanders & Specialist Officers carried out a reconnaissance of the HAZEBROUCK Defence System. A football match was played with the 21st Middlesex Battn on the R.A.F. ground the Battn winning by 3 goals to nil.	W4

Army Form C. 2118.

WAR DIARY
or
INTELLIGENCE SUMMARY.
(Erase heading not required.)

Place	Date	Hour	Summary of Events and Information	Remarks and references to Appendices
STAPLE O.30.a.2.2	22.5.18		The Orderly Officer conducted the Parade at 10 a.m. & Supervised the following parades. Bayonet Fighting, Gas Instruction. The Commanding Officer + Adjutant mounted the HONDEGHEM Switch.	GH
STAPLE O.30.a.2.2	23.5.18		Company Commanders + Specialist Officers reconnoitred the HONDEGHEM Switch. The remainder of the Training Establishment carried on with P.T. + Bay. F. Musketry and General Musketry	GH
STAPLE O.30.a.2.2	24.5.18		Inspection Parade at 10 a.m. under the Orderly Officer. A Battalion Guest & Dinner was held at M/4 Kite Balloon Section Headquarters + the Brigade Staff + members of the units in the Brigade were present.	GH
STAPLE O.30.a.2.2	25.5.18		The Orderly Officer inspected the Staff Parade at 10 a.m. Coy Company Commanders & the Senior Officers staff of Courses.	GH
STAPLE O.30.a.2.2	26.5.18		The Commanding Officer inspected the personnel of the Training Establishment at 10 a.m. The men were paid at 2 p.m.	GH

Army Form C. 2118

WAR DIARY
or
INTELLIGENCE SUMMARY

(Erase heading not required.)

Instructions regarding War Diaries and Intelligence Summaries are contained in F.S. Regs., Part II. and the Staff Manual respectively. Title Pages will be prepared in manuscript.

Place	Date	Hour	Summary of Events and Information	Remarks and references to Appendices
STAPLE. O.30.a.3.2	27.5.18		Inspection at 10 a.m. by the Orderly Officer. The Commanding Officer proceeded on leave to U.K. & Capt. J.F. Lawrence took over Command from this date.	O.I.f.
STAPLE. O.30.a.3.2	28.5.18		Inspection at 10 a.m. by the Orderly Officer. Parades as follows: Physical Training, Bayonet Fighting, Guard Mounting, Semaphore Training.	
STAPLE. O.30.a.3.2	29.5.18		The Commanding Officer & Company Commanders reconnoitred the Defence Line in front of STAPLES. A number of the Training Establishment were innoculated.	O.I.f.
STAPLE. O.30.a.3.2	30.5.18		The Commdg Officer & all Officers reconnoitred the Defence Line in front of STAPLES. There were no parades for the men owing to the majority of the men having been innoculated the day previous.	O.I.f.
STAPLE. O.30.a.3.2	31.5.18		Inspection at 10 a.m. by the Orderly Officer. The C.O. & Coy Commdrs reconnoitred the General Defence Area east of around STAPLES.	O.I.f.

Lawrence
Capt.
a/Commanding 1/8th Bn the Welsh Regt.

Army Form C. 2118.

WAR DIARY
or
INTELLIGENCE SUMMARY.
(Erase heading not required.)

18 W6L Bty

Vol 25

WAR DIARY
FOR
1/18" JUNE 1918

258
inshed

Army Form C. 2118.

WAR DIARY
or
INTELLIGENCE SUMMARY.
(Erase heading not required.)

Instructions regarding War Diaries and Intelligence Summaries are contained in F. S. Regs., Part II. and the Staff Manual respectively. Title pages will be prepared in manuscript.

Place	Date	Hour	Summary of Events and Information	Remarks and references to Appendices
STAPLE	1.6.18		The Transport Establishment paraded at 10.0 am for inspection by the Commanding Officer, afterwards all officers reconnoitred the HONDEGHEM SWITCH N0 2 Sector	
"	2.6.18		Inspection at 10.0 am by the Orderly Officer. The men were paid during the morning	
"	3.6.18		Capt J.J. Lawrence MC relinquished command of the Battn on being attached to Brigade for duty & Capt G.H. Jones MC assumed command from this date. The General Establishment paraded for Inspection. Signalling, P.T. & B.F. under the Orderly Officer	
"	4.6.18		Inspection of grooms kit & accoutrements at 9.0 am by the 2.I.C. The Orderly Officer inspected the Parade at 10.0 am. The C.O. & all officers reconnoitred positions for Brigade & Battn Headqrs in the HONDEGHEM SWITCH, N0 2 SECTOR.	
"	5.6.18		Inspection at 10.0 am by the Orderly Officer. The C.O. & one Coy Commander reconnoitred for Suitable transport lines in the Corps Area. HONDEGHEM SWITCH N0 2 Sector	
"	6.6.18		Inspection at 9.45 am. The following training programme was carried out – P.T. & B.F. & Ceremonial Guard mounting. Gas Drill	
"	7.6.18		Inspection at 9.45 am by the Orderly Officer. Parades were as follows P.T. & B.F. Lewis Gun Instruction. Gas drill & Signalling Instruction	

Army Form C. 2118.

WAR DIARY
or
INTELLIGENCE SUMMARY.
(Erase heading not required.)

Instructions regarding War Diaries and Intelligence Summaries are contained in F. S. Regs., Part II. and the Staff Manual respectively. Title pages will be prepared in manuscript.

Place	Date	Hour	Summary of Events and Information	Remarks and references to Appendices
STAPLE	8.6.18		The 2/C.O. inspected the Personnel of the Training Establishment at 10 am.	
"	9.6.18		All Officers reconnoitred the HONDEGHEM SWITCH, No 2. Sub-area work the men at maintaining the water supply & condition of the roads.	
STUYVER N.17. b.07.10	10.6.18		The Battalion moved to N.7.b.00.10 + marched thither.	
"	11.6.18		Inspection at 10.0 am by the Orderly Officer. All Officers reconnoitred Ground allotted to No 2. Sub of HONDEGHEM SWITCH.	
"	12.6.18		The men halted at ARNEKE at 9 am. Officers reconnoitred the BALEMBERG Line 9.0.5 Sub.	
"	13.6.18		The Orderly Officer inspected the parade at 9.45 am. Coy Officers v the 2/C.O reconnoitred the BALEMBERG LINE. Lieut Col. W.E. Brown D.S.O. M.C. returned from leave & took of our Command after Batn.	
"	14.6.18		Inspection at 9.45 am by the Orderly Officer. The men paraded for instruction in Signalling, Lewis guns + Gas Drill. The C.O. + Adjt reconnoitred the BALEMBERG LINE in the afternoon.	
ST MOMELIN [Bois-du-HAM]	15.6.18		The Battn moved from STUYVER Area N.7. b.00.10 at 10.0 am proceeding by march route to Bois-du-HAM – ST MOMELIN. Arrived at 1.30 p.m.	

WAR DIARY
or
INTELLIGENCE SUMMARY.

(Erase heading not required.)

Army Form C. 2118.

Place	Date	Hour	Summary of Events and Information	Remarks and references to Appendices
St. MONTEUIL [Bois du Ham]	16.6.18		The Battn received warning orders to prepare to embark for ENGLAND. The day was spent in preparing for the move.	A/.
"	17.6.18		The Battn received definite orders to move on this date + marched to ST OMER at 8.0 am, left ST. OMER at 10.43 am for BOULOGNE. An officer of the 11th Division met the unit the Battn at BOULOGNE.	A/.

[Signature]
Lieut-Col.
Commanding 18th (S) Battn. The Welsh Regt.

www.ingramcontent.com/pod-product-compliance
Lightning Source LLC
Chambersburg PA
CBHW081528160426
43191CB00011B/1708